You Inspire Me

A True Story of Unconditional Love

Neda Azadivatan, DDS

SP
Sunshine Press, LLC

You Inspire Me

A True Story of Unconditional Love

Neda Azadivatan, DDS

FIRST EDITION

Manufactured in the United States of America

Paperback ISBN: 979-8-9914672-0-9
eBook ISBN: 979-8-9914672-1-6

Library of Congress Control Number:

SP
Sunshine Press, LLC

Contents

To my five beautiful children:
Kian, Kamran, Cyrus, Leila, and Sia.
I love you all very much
and am profoundly blessed
to be your mom.

Chapter 1
The Most Severe Form

"UNFORTUNATELY, I'M AFRAID THERE is no cure. All that's available is supportive therapy."

Dr. Parvez's words didn't register at first. Supportive therapy? What did that even mean? No cure? How could that be? There was a cure. There had to be a cure.

Kian was only nine weeks old. He'd been a perfectly healthy, adorable, baby boy, and I was completely enamored. Kian had smiling eyes, and his cooing sounds had made my heart melt. But at his eight-week checkup a week before, the pediatrician had said, until Dr. Parvez's words, the most disturbing thing I had ever heard: "There's something seriously wrong with this child."

"What do you mean?" I asked.

The pediatrician lifted Kian's little arms and let them go. They fell lifelessly beside him. My mind raced. Kian was my first child. I had dozens and dozens of pictures of him. Arms raised, hands out, legs moving. But had he been as

1

active lately? I couldn't be sure. He was just a little baby, after all.

"I want you to take him to Westchester Medical Center," the pediatrician continued, frowning. And then he added this: "Take him now."

Westchester Medical Center was about an hour south of our home in Rhinebeck, New York. My mother was with me, and we put Kian in the car and drove there with me crying most of the way. I called my husband, telling him he needed to meet me at the medical center, but he didn't want to leave work, ignoring my concern, telling me it was probably no big deal. Maybe some sort of vitamin deficiency. But he hadn't seen the look in the doctor's face. Ultimately, Patrick drove down later that evening. My mother and I would still be there because we were there not only that day, but for the entire next week.

Kian had a battery of tests done. It was brutal. He was awakened early every morning to be picked and probed. He'd cry hysterically while I watched, feeling helpless. Groups of resident physicians would come by with their instructor lecturing about all the possible things that might be wrong with Kian. The residents could see me out of the corner of their eyes, but I noticed that they were careful not to make direct eye contact, pretending I wasn't there.

One attending physician wanted to give Kian a spinal tap, but he could give me no good reason other than, "Everybody that comes through my ER gets blood work, urine analysis, and a spinal tap."

"Not my baby," I said, imagining the hollow needle impaled between the bones of Kian's spine. "If you tell me it's a matter of life or death, okay, but if all you want to do is let these kids practice how to do a spinal tap, this baby's mom is not going to allow it."

The attending physician rolled his eyes and walked out, the group of residents trailing behind, still not making eye contact.

I didn't eat that week, losing all the weight I had gained during the pregnancy. I didn't sleep either. Finally, Dr. Parvez, a pediatric neurologist, having pored over the results of all the tests, delivered the diagnosis. Kian had spinal muscular atrophy—SMA, a degenerative genetic disorder that affects the nerve cells in the spinal cord that control movement. SMA causes certain muscles to become weak and waste away. And that's when I'd asked about the treatment. The cure.

All that's available is supportive therapy.

My mind was paralyzed with questions and emotions. I tried to form words. I wanted to know what "supportive" meant. Support for what? For how long? Was Kian going to die? What did this disorder do exactly? What did it mean?

In a monotone voice, the doctor pressed on, anticipating my questions. "He's under six months," he said. "That means he has the most severe form. He will not be able to roll, sit, walk. Eventually, he will lose the ability to swallow and he'll need a feeding tube inserted into his stomach. He'll need continual suctioning of his secretions to keep from choking. At some point, he'll lose the muscle capacity to breathe and he'll need to be placed on a ventilator." Then he paused, giving me a moment to absorb the gut-wrenching blows, before saying, "The prognosis is not good. I'm afraid your son will most likely not survive past his second birthday."

I don't remember what else the doctor said. He talked at length about SMA, but it was all a blur. I recall the room spinning. It was hard to breathe. I remember feeling as if the building was crumbling down upon me, as though I were being buried alive.

"Take him home and take lots of pictures," Dr. Parvez finally said. I do remember that much. "Give him lots of love," he concluded.

My next memory is wandering zombie-like down the hospital hallways. Little by little, certain words the doctor had said started to register. Degenerative. Choking. Ventilator. *Your son will not survive past his second birthday.* We were already at stage 2 baby food. Kian loved his sweet potato. And soon he wasn't going to be able to swallow? But he'd been so healthy. The pregnancy had gone smoothly. All the doctor visits and the ultrasounds. "He has a strong kick!" one of the technicians had observed.

Finally, I stumbled across the chapel. It was 4 a.m., November 11, 2006. No one else was around. There was a dim light and some candles burning. And then, in the deathly quiet of the room, it all came out at once. I sobbed, screamed, prayed. I found myself angry at God. Why Kian? *Why?*

Vaguely, I wondered what I was going to do, how I was going to go on. It seemed impossible. Later, I would come to realize that in that chapel, I had started the grieving process. But Kian was not dead. He was still very much alive. It was too soon to grieve. Something must have told me this because in that moment, in that quiet chapel, I suddenly wanted nothing more than to be with my son. I rose and walked out of the chapel and hurried toward Kian's room. I needed to see him. I needed to see my beautiful baby boy.

Chapter 2

Always Moving

I HAD WANTED TO give Kian a wonderful childhood. That was the most important thing in the world for me. My own was not without its difficulties.

In 1974, when I was four, my mother took me and my half-brother, Cyrus, to see my father's grave. It's one of my very first memories. We spent four hours on a bus and walked three miles through the heat of Tehran to get there. Three years earlier, when I was seventeen months old, my father had taken his own life. He was thirty-two. But that's not what I'd been told. My mother had told me he'd died in an automobile accident. After the visit to the grave, I found out the truth from one of the kids in the neighborhood. A boy named Sharam said, "Your dad was a heroin addict and killed himself, and my mom and dad don't want us to play with you."

I was so mad, I picked up a metal pipe and hit Sharam over the head with it. My mother beat me practically senseless when she found out, stopping only when Cyrus intervened. But in the midst of it, after I'd been crying to her why I'd hit Sharam, after repeating his accusation, my mother screamed out, "*Yes*, he was a druggie! He killed himself so you wouldn't grow up to be ashamed of him!"

For years I felt responsible for my father's death.

Their marriage had been my mother's second. She was first married when she was sixteen to a man named Jafar who was thirty-five years her senior. It was an arranged marriage, not uncommon in Iran back then. The couple would have four children, but my mother would leave Jafar from time to time. She was young and she was unhappy. One time, she met my father and she left Jafar for good.

Later, as I grew up, she would tell me more about my father. "He was the love of my life," she'd say. "He was my everything." My father had been in a car accident; that much was true. But the accident didn't kill him. The painkillers did that. He'd severely injured his arm in the accident and surgery to repair it did not go well, probably botched by an incompetent doctor. He was in constant pain. And terribly depressed. A prominent engineer, he could no longer focus on his job. He could no longer support his family, something he had done since he was a boy as the oldest son in his household. He'd even helped put one of his brothers through college. Now he was helpless. His addiction to his painkillers grew. Eventually, morphine turned to heroin.

As my mother would tell me about him, her eyes would brim with tears. "I threatened many times to leave him," she would say. "He tried to quit a few times, but he could never stay sober for long. We would sometimes go days without food in the house. Even when I was pregnant with you, I had no prenatal care. And after you were born, there was no money to buy you formula."

Finally, my mother left my father and reconciled with Jafar under the condition that he would adopt me. Telling me this, she made it sound like she only did this for me, as if it were some noble sacrifice, but I could never help wondering if her leaving my father was a way of running from her problems, not dissimilar to what my father was doing with his drug use.

We moved in with Jafar and my two half-brothers, Cyrus, twelve years old, and Kiavosh, fourteen. The other two half-siblings were my half-brother Sia and my half-sister Pari, but both were older and had moved out of the apartment, even out of the country. Sia had traveled to the United States and was a student at the University of Miami. Pari was a professional ballerina in Italy.

It was a two-bedroom apartment for the five of us, no bigger than a thousand square feet. It was the seventies and the apartment had trendy wallpaper with large, brown flowers, and wall-to-wall carpeting, although we had a couple of Persian rugs laid down over top. The kitchen was so small that no more than two people could fit into it at any given time. There was one bathroom with a toilet that was more or less a hole in the floor. Western toilets were a luxury. But I loved our apartment. It seemed big enough to me. And it was on the top floor of our four-story building, giving us a beautiful view. The apartment looked out at the Alborz Mountains. Even better, behind the building there were swings and seesaws.

Kia and Cyrus both made me feel at home. Cyrus, especially. Jafar insisted that they take good care of their little sister, and Cyrus took it to heart. We would become very close and I would always know that I had a big brother who would protect me.

By the time we moved into the apartment, Jafar was old and frail, but gentle and kind. He was an educated, principled man, surrounded by books. He had university degrees in political science and accounting, and in the 1950s, he had been governor of the Baluchistan province of Iran. But being governor hadn't translated to wealth for Jafar. He was a true servant of the people, highly respected and always pulling for the underdog. My father came around a couple of times and, on what would be his last visit,

Jafar encouraged him to get help, even offering him money. Then he assured him he would take good care of me and that my father was welcome to come back any time.

It was not long after that when my father decided to end his life. Much later, I would learn that he drove four hours to a beach resort on the Caspian Sea where he took cyanide. His body was found two days later, his hand clutching photographs of my mother and me. My mother refused to see the body, though I never knew why. Perhaps out of anger. As a little girl, I imagined that because she hadn't actually seen him dead, my father might have still been alive somewhere. Maybe the authorities had made a mistake in identifying the body. Maybe he'd return one day. I even dreamed one night that he came to pick me up at school.

But Jafar was the only father I would know. Old and retired, he spent most of his time at home. He would sit me on his lap and tell me stories. I was his little girl and he was my daddy. Yes, he was old, but he made me feel loved and safe. Then one night, Jafar died in his sleep of a stroke. I was heartbroken.

My mother, meanwhile, had to find a way to support us. There was Jafar's monthly social security check, but it wasn't close to enough. Though she couldn't read or write, my mother was determined to somehow find a way, starting a few weeks after Jafar's funeral. She sold our Persian rugs and most of our furniture. Our little apartment never looked emptier, and there was a sadness that hung over the place, especially since the absence of Jafar was so palpable to me. Then she took a housekeeping job at a local hotel and cleaned the homes of wealthy Americans on weekends. She often complained of pain in her overworked hands. But she still couldn't make ends meet and ended up renting out our other bedroom to a mother and her grown daughter. We had enough to pay the bills, but it meant four of us sleeping in one bedroom, sheets and comforters laid out on the floor. The kitchen and bathroom were shared areas.

The daughter's name was Minu and she worked night shifts as a nurse at a local hospital. I was curious about her work, and Minu took me with her sometimes and I would spend the night there. I loved the hospital. It was clean, and the staff all seemed very busy and engaged. The physicians, with their clipboards, and stethoscopes hanging around their necks, seemed so important and vital. From the age of four, I decided I wanted to be a doctor. I didn't know what kind, but I wanted to do important work, too. This came as welcomed news to my mother who kept telling me how important it was to have a professional career. She said so many times that she wished she'd had an education. "You listen to me," she would say. "You *have* to get an education. I do not want you to end up like me, working as a maid, scrubbing toilets and cleaning up after others."

But my mother, despite her lack of education, or maybe because of it, was a determined, strong woman. She was not going to let us lose the apartment. The second strongest woman I knew was my grandmother on my father's side. Every weekend, Cyrus and I would visit her. She and my mother never really made peace for some reason, but both cared for me very much. My grandmother—Monie, as I called her—had been a single mother. Her husband had been executed. She told us of how, in the middle of the night, when she was pregnant with my father's little sister, government guards had come to the house, accusing my grandfather of being a communist, which was true. They took him and hung him in the center of town, then dragged his body through the streets to show people what would happen to them if they spoke up for freedom. It was my grandfather who had provided us with our last name, changing my family name before his death to Azadivatan, which means "freedom of the homeland."

Of course, this was back in the Shah days. Shah Mohammad Reza Pahlavi had come to power in a US-backed coup in 1953. He became increasingly power-hungry, surrounding himself with a secret police force and doing away with anyone deemed a threat to his regime. The Shah, promising a more democratic society, became instead a veritable dictator.

I remember Grandma Monie as a warm, loving woman whose smile would light up a room in spite of the fact that she had no teeth and refused to wear her dentures. She would read me stories and tell me I was her favorite grandchild. I reminded her very much of my dad, she would say. "Someday, Neda," she'd tell me, "you will realize everything on your own. God has a plan for you. Never doubt that your father loved you very much. He is watching you from above. Always remember that." I took it literally, believing my dad lived in the clouds or on the moon. I would look up into the sky and imagine him seeing me. Looking back, I marvel at Grandma Monie's strength. Her husband was murdered by the government, she raised five children on her own, and she endured the loss of a son by suicide. And yet she never lost her resolve or her good nature.

In 1978, my mother made an announcement. We were moving to Italy to live with my half-sister Pari and her daughter Patrizia who was two years younger than me. Things were not good in Iran and there was nothing to keep my mother there. We needed a new start. Pari had just divorced; she had money and could support us. But first, we were going to Miami to see Sia, and Kia who had also moved to Miami by then. We would spend the summer there and then my mother and I would fly to Italy, with Cyrus staying in the US.

Our twelve-hour flight from Tehran to JFK was my first time on an airplane, a two-level Pan Am plane with flight attendants in crisp blue uniforms with little hats who gave me coloring books and crayons. From JFK it was on to Miami, which turned out to be a family reunion of sorts. Pari met us there, staying for a few days before returning to Italy where we would join her at the end of the summer. I'd met her when I was little, before she'd moved to Italy, but had no recollection of her. She was beautiful—five-five with short brown hair, olive skin, a ballerina figure, full lips, and a bright smile. But she was cold and intimidating. The first thing she said to me was, "Why do you talk like a little kitten? Can't you speak up?" Then she turned to my mother and said, "When I was her age, I was taking care of three younger brothers. She is eight but sounds like a three-year-old."

But the summer was magical. We went to the movies where I saw my childhood crush, John Travolta, in *Grease*. We visited Disney World. Cyrus bought me a bicycle with a white banana seat. I got a Barbie Doll with a princess gown. I watched color TV for the first time, mesmerized by the images of American television. Sia's apartment complex had a pool and I swam every day with friends I made in the complex. I learned some English—"How are you," "I love ice cream," "Shit."

I didn't want the summer to end, but in late August, my mother and I were off to Milan. Pari lived in a beautiful apartment in an exclusive neighborhood. She worked across the border in Switzerland and would come home to visit on weekends. I learned that she had started out in a ballet company, then had been a runway model in Paris, and was now working in Swiss nightclubs. When she came home, she always had different people with her and the apartment was a madhouse of grown-ups. She spent very little time with her daughter, but she made good money and we were all well taken care of.

Patrizia, technically my niece, became more like a sister to me. She couldn't speak Farsi and at first, I couldn't speak a word of Italian, but within no time, we were communicating, somehow understanding each other as only kids can. Meanwhile, Pari hired an Iranian college student to teach me Italian. Between him and Patrizia, I learned quickly. In a year, I was enrolled in an elementary school and making friends. Iran seemed like a lifetime ago.

But then the country of my birth came back to me every evening on the news. I was nine during the Iranian Revolution of 1979. The Shah was deposed and the Ayatollah Ruhollah Khomeini came to power, putting in place a theocratic government—the Islamic Republic of Iran. Khomeini was now the "Supreme Leader." On TV, we watched as millions demonstrated in the streets of Tehran. Schools were closed. Revolutionary students took over the American embassy, taking hostages, and American flags were burned everywhere.

Kia and Cyrus took the revolution to mean better times for Iran. The autocratic Shah was gone, along with his authoritarian government. This new government represented the promise of better times. Kia had earned his degree in political science by then and he and Cyrus decided that they could be a part of the nation's reform, their concern for the people a direct result of their father's influence. They went back. My mother wasn't sold on the idea of a better future for Iran, but she decided she had to be there for her sons. For me, however, she knew I was better off in Milan. She sat me down and said, "You have to be a big girl and stay here. Pari has agreed to enroll you in a very prestigious boarding school. You'll have everything you could ask for. You'll have opportunities here that do not exist in Iran. And as soon as things settle down there, I'll come visit you here."

When my mother left in the summer of 1980, I cried for days. I couldn't eat and I couldn't sleep. My world had been turned upside down. "You're such a crybaby!" Pari would shout at me without a shred of sympathy. "When I was your age, I dreamed of a life like this!"

Things didn't get any better. One time I even overheard Pari telling one of her model friends that she didn't especially like children. I asked her one day why she was so mean and she responded with, "Get over here you little brat!" and then held up her hand as if she were going to slap me across the face. Instead, she picked up the phone and called our mother, telling her she couldn't take having me there anymore. I was a constant nuisance.

My mother agreed that it would be for the best if I returned to Iran. Pari couldn't wait to get me on the next plane to Tehran. I would always wonder, looking back, what my life would have been like had I stayed in Europe and attended boarding school in Italy. Had Pari been more open toward me. What might my relationship with Patrizia and the rest of the family have been like?

My mom, Cyrus, and Kia were at the Tehran airport and I cried when we were reunited, so happy was I to be with them again. But I learned quickly how much Iran had changed since the revolution. I now had to dress in accordance with Islamic code. I had to cover my head with a chador, pretend to be a good Muslim, and praise the Ayatollah. I was made to study the Koran, which was in Arabic, meaning that I had to learn Arabic.

This state of affairs was not at all what Cyrus and Kia had anticipated. Now, with the country out from under the control of the Shah, they had hoped for more free-dom—democracy, freedom of speech and press, a sepa-ration of religion and government. The new regime was none of those things. Worse, their beliefs put them in dan-ger. Neighbors were turning on each other, making it as bad or worse as when the Shah was in power. Fear pervaded everything.

In October of 1983, my brothers' best friend, Ebbi, was arrested. His brother, Majeed, came to our house early one morning to tell us, and to warn us. "You guys have to get out of here," he told my brothers. We all knew why. Ebbi had come under suspicion, and there was no telling how much torture he would be able to withstand before he started giving up names of comrades. My mother started crying hysterically. "They are going to kill that poor child!" she wailed.

My brothers lit out for our grandparents' house two hours south of Tehran, knowing it could provide only temporary safety. They needed to get out of Iran. But people perceived as political enemies were often executed trying to flee the country, meaning it wasn't safe to stay and it wasn't safe to leave. In November, my mother took a trip to Zahedan, close to the Pakistani border. Through her brother-in-law, she had contacts that could help my brothers escape, though to this day I do not know who they were. She left with my brothers while I stayed at my grandparents with explicit instructions not to talk to anybody about what was happening. We worried for four long days before my mother finally opened the door of my grandparents' house and walked inside with a look of relief on her face. She hugged me and whispered in my ear, "Your brothers are now safe in Pakistan."

Meanwhile, things got only worse in Iran. In addition to the problems from within, there were soon problems from without. I started hearing the name Saddam Hussein. Iran was under attack from Iraq. Saddam hadn't liked what he saw with the Iranian Revolution, the leadership toppled. He feared the expansion of revolution in his own country. When Tehran started to get bombed in 1985, my mother had had enough. "There is no future for you here," she told me. But I had friends, even something of a boyfriend by then, although because of the strict enforcement of Sharia law, we had to keep our little puppy-love romance a secret. It seemed all I had done in my young life was move. I was always moving. And now I was moving again.

My mother sold our house and all our furniture and we took a bus to the Turkish border. The Tehran airport, targeted by the Iraqis, was closed. But there were so many people leaving that we had to wait three days at the border before we could get processed into Turkey. We went to Ankara, then Istanbul. Then we went to the US consulate and procured three-month visas to the States and were soon on our way to Miami where Cyrus and Kia had returned after having slipped into Pakistan. I was coming back to the US. Hopefully to stay.

Chapter 3
Dark Cloud

WE LANDED IN MIAMI on June 5, 1985. It was hot and humid, and you could see the steam rising off the asphalt from an earlier rain. Cyrus and Kia were waiting for us. Cyrus was driving his new silver Volkswagen, his first new car, and he took us to the three-bedroom, two-bath townhouse they rented. Sia was still in Miami, too. He had married a Colombian girl named Emma whom he had met while studying business at the University of Miami. Now, he had an automobile electronics business and was doing well, living in a fashionable apartment on Brickell Avenue.

For the first few days at the townhouse, all I did was sleep and visit the complex's pool, but then Cyrus drove me to Miami-Dade Community College to enroll me in an English class. I had three months to learn the language before school would start in the fall.

A few weeks later, in July of 1985, we welcomed another family member. It seemed Pari had now tired of having her own daughter around. Truthfully, Patrizia had become more than a handful. She'd failed seventh grade, had been caught smoking, and had been expelled from the boarding school. Pari was at her wit's end. She flew over with Patrizia, believing that if she left her with us, maybe I'd have a positive influence on her.

I hadn't seen Patrizia in six years and was stunned by her transformation. She wore high heels, was dressed like Madonna, had short hair with bleached bangs, had multiple earrings, and her face was caked with makeup. This was not the girl I had seen last in Milan. Pari stayed a few days and flew back to Italy, her daughter now our responsibility.

Mom was hard on Patrizia. No more high heels. No more makeup. No more dressing like Madonna. Patrizia enrolled in my English class and before long, she was a regular thirteen-year-old again. That fall, we attended Glades Junior High, me in ninth grade, Patrizia in eighth. The following year, I moved on to the high school. We were both adjusting to life in America, but Patrizia wasn't adjusting as well. Mom continued to be tough on her, even criticizing her to the point where Cyrus would step in and defend her.

Patrizia stayed with us for almost two years. Then, one afternoon, I went to the bus stop to get her, but she wasn't on the bus. We called the school and learned that Patrizia had attended her classes, but nobody had any idea where she'd gone afterward. We called the police. Two days came and went. We posted flyers. The police questioned her friends, but nobody knew anything of her whereabouts. I lay awake at night, listening for her, hoping to hear her coming through the front door.

Then my mother noticed that her jewelry box was missing. The police found Patrizia. She was with friends and had called Pari, telling her she wanted to come home. Pari acquiesced and bought her a plane ticket. So ended Patrizia's stay with us, leaving us all a little hurt, and leaving Mom furious. I was more hurt than anyone. I felt betrayed, and yet I couldn't help but wonder if maybe, in Patrizia's eyes, I had somehow betrayed her. Why had she not come to me and confided in me? Why did she not at least say goodbye to me? Whatever was going through her mind, why was she afraid to trust me? Later, I would be haunted by these thoughts, thoughts that I had somehow failed Patrizia.

Meanwhile, my high school years passed and my childhood in Iran faded further and further into the background. I loved America. I loved Miami, and even stuck around after high school, getting a bachelor's degree in microbiology at the University of Miami in 1994. Cyrus, true to form, helped me make college a reality, providing me an allowance and even buying me a car.

While at UM, I'd had a root canal done and found myself fascinated by the process, probably not a common reaction for a patient undergoing the procedure. But I'd never forgotten those nights I'd spent as a child in the hospital, dreaming of a career in the medical field. My future came into focus. I was going to be a dentist.

For my post-graduate work, I decided I wanted to get away from home and see more of the US. And I wanted to go to a prestigious school. I applied to Boston University, NYU, and Columbia and visited them all. My college grades had been good and I knew I stood a good chance of acceptance. In fact, they all accepted me. I chose Columbia, enamored by the fact that it was an Ivy League school. Cyrus warned me about New York City and leaving home. "You won't like it," he said. "You'll want to come back home."

Six months later, I proved him right. This was the mid-'90s and Spanish Harlem, where Columbia was located, was not an especially great area of New York. Plus, I had trouble making friends and felt as if I didn't fit in. I missed Miami; I missed my family. I came home, forfeiting $25,000 in tuition in the process.

Back home, I took a job as a dental assistant in a multi-specialty office, one specialty of which was periodontics, the treatment of gums and the bones that support the teeth. The field looked interesting and I could suddenly see myself as a periodontist. I decided to try school again. I still wanted to be in New York; I hadn't lost my fascination with the city or my interest in getting away from home. Or maybe I felt as if I needed to prove to myself I could make it there. Either way, I figured it would be good for me to try. This time, I opted for NYU, and it turned out to be the right decision.

At NYU, I made friends in the dental school, some of whom became friends for life. Today, we might not see each other often, but when we do, it's as though no time has passed. At dental school, we looked out for each other. We enjoyed the city life. We studied hard, and we played hard. I dated, too. A lot of jerks, as it turned out, but some good guys, as well. I was growing. I was learning about myself. And I was enjoying life.

But none of it came cheap. By the time I was interning at Mount Sinai hospital, in my last semester, I was out of money. I was strung out on student loans and had no source of income. I was forced out of my apartment and had to move in with a friend. I pawned some of my jewelry to buy food. Finally, I realized that with my financial situation, I would not be able to continue. I was going to have to quit and find work. In one final, desperate move, I called Pari and asked for help. "This bank is closed," she snapped. "You need to find a job."

I went to Dean Fredrick Moore's office and explained that I would need to take some time off, telling him of my precarious economic circumstances. The dean listened and then told me to come back in a few days with everything related to my financial situation, including copies of my bills. When I returned, he explained that he had managed to convince the school to give me $6,000 in grant money. I started to cry. With Dean Moore's help, and the help of my friend Galina Yankulin, who cosigned a loan for me, I was going to make it after all.

I finished my last year and graduated in May of 2000, deciding to stick around the New York area. I entered a one-year residency program at Flushing Hospital in Queens, and shared a nearby apartment with my friend Sherri from NYU. That summer, I met Michael, an ER resident from Long Island. We had a lot in common and could relate easily to each other. Michael was from a struggling family. His father was an alcoholic and divorced from his mother. He was the only one from his family to attend graduate school and had paid his own way. We began seeing a lot of each other, and I found myself falling in love.

Flushing Hospital, meanwhile, was an absolute nightmare. The residents were berated continually and treated like indentured servants. The problem came from the director on down, and I couldn't wait to finish. After that year, I was scheduled to attend the University of Medicine and Dentistry of New Jersey (UMDNJ) in Newark for their three-year periodontics program. But first I had to survive Flushing. This was not easy. At one point, the director, infamous for harassing residents, called me into his office and threatened to contact the assistant to the program director of UMDNJ, jeopardizing my acceptance there. My chest tightened and I couldn't speak. I walked out of his office and promptly fell to the floor. My next memory is of being treated in the ER. I'd had convulsions and was hyperventilating. It was a severe panic attack, something I'd never experienced before. When it was determined what set it off, the director was reprimanded for his threats and I was never harassed again. Flushing got a little better after that.

Michael and I kept seeing each other. I met his family and friends, and when I thought of my future, I thought of Michael and me together. Marriage seemed like a foregone conclusion. My career path was still up in the air, but I felt as if my love life was at least secure.

Then, after Michael's residency, he took a job placement in North Carolina. We hadn't discussed it. Of course, if I had to, I would forego UMDNJ and move to North Carolina with Michael, but I was surprised he hadn't thought to consult me. When I questioned him, I found out why.

"It would never work out," he said.

"What do you mean?" I asked. "What wouldn't work out?"

"Us," he said.

"What—"

"I don't love you, Neda. I'm sorry."

And that was that. I was devastated. How could I have so misread our relationship?

Finally, my time at Flushing came to an end and I couldn't wait to get out of Queens. It was full of heartache for me. I was accepted into the UMDNJ periodontic program, and I should have been ecstatic, but after Michael had dumped me, I felt like I was living under a dark cloud. I moved to Jersey City and rented the first floor of a house in a rundown neighborhood. It was all I could afford. Quickly, I discovered that UMDNJ was just as nightmarish as Flushing. The faculty was old and apathetic and they seemed to get their kicks out of grilling and humiliating the residents.

I found a friend in one of them, however. Carol Brownstein was the assistant to the program director, ironically the very person the director at Flushing had threatened to call to keep me from getting in. I spent many hours in Carol's office crying about my life, and she kept encouraging me. "Periodontics is not easy," she'd say, "but you are a very determined girl and I know you'll make it. When I was going through the program, my husband walked out on me, leaving me with two kids. Believe me, if I could do it, so can you." I wouldn't have made it without Carol.

There were others who helped. Men dominated the residency program, but I became friends with two very goal-oriented, strong-willed women. Melissa Pecorraro was in my year, and Katie Teevan was a year behind. The three of us formed a sisterhood that would help me get through the next three years. We inspired and encouraged each other. Sometimes, we were just there for each other, doing nothing but listening and caring.

Meanwhile, my financial problems weren't going away and, in fact, were only getting worse. I had $350,000 worth of student debt from NYU, and I knew by the time I'd leave UMDNJ in three years, I'd accumulate another $200,000, adding up to an imposing half million. I took a Saturday job in the Bronx at a dental office, even though it was against UMDNJ rules. I had no choice.

Then one day the dark cloud got darker. Cyrus called. Patrizia's life in Milan had gotten worse. She had remained rebellious and unruly. Pari, having done everything in her power to help her daughter, had finally decided to try tough love: she cut off communication with Patrizia and they'd gone their separate ways. Patrizia had had no place to stay. She'd been depressed. She'd been in counseling where she met a friend who invited Patrizia out to dinner with her boyfriend. They took Patrizia for a ride outside of the city. Then they strangled her, taking her cell phone and Omega watch.

Patrizia was dead.

We all asked ourselves what more we could have done. Patrizia died, brutally and alone, at the age of twenty-nine, but I would forever see her in my mind as that fifteen-year-old who'd left one day without telling me goodbye, without giving me the chance to hug her, and tell her how special she was, and how loved by all of us.

I kept getting up in the mornings and going to UMD-NJ, but I felt numb. I felt no purpose in life. I felt lonely. I spiraled into a depression and spent the next year in therapy and taking anti-depressants.

Back in Miami, Patrizia's death was having even more of an impact on Cyrus. The two had been close. Cyrus had kept in touch with Patrizia over the years, privy to all she had been through and her death hit him especially hard. I started getting calls from family and from Cyrus's friends: Cyrus was beginning to act erratically. There was talk of drug use. Then, in the midst of everything, his wife left him and filed for divorce. He teetered on the edge of a nervous breakdown.

I flew to Miami, and with the support of the family, I had Cyrus temporarily committed. It was an agonizing decision to have to make, but it was the right one; he was exhibiting symptoms of schizophrenia and had become a danger to himself. But the action, taken out of love, and concern for Cyrus's very life, would create a wedge between us. Cyrus would recover, and our relationship would survive, but it would never be the same.

Chapter 4

Mother

THE NEWS SEEMED TO keep getting worse. One day, my mom called to tell me that my thirty-nine-year-old uncle had died of a massive heart attack. He'd been visiting from Iran, spending time with his kids in New York. His kids—my cousins—were ages ten and twelve and lived with my uncle's ex-wife, my Aunt Carleen. After spending time there, my uncle had gone to Miami to visit friends. One morning he went for a jog, returned to his friend's house, and fell down dead in their kitchen.

Mom wanted me to go to Miami to help out Aunt Carleen who had flown down with my cousins. The next day, I flew to Miami and tended to the kids while Aunt Carleen took care of the funeral arrangements. I stuck around for the funeral, but when I drove my rental car to the funeral home, I couldn't bring myself to go inside. My uncle had been young and vibrant, and I didn't want to imagine him any other way. How could he be so alive one moment and then dead the next? Nothing made sense. I sat in the car and cried.

Back in Jersey City, I was depressed, lonely, overworked, and in crippling debt. At the end of my first year at UMD-NJ, I took an apartment in Hoboken, rooming with a first-year dental student named Callie. The move was my therapist's idea. I needed a new environment, somewhere safer and more stable. Somewhere to give me a new perspective, perhaps a fresh start. I also left my job in the Bronx and got a better one at a practice in Manhattan for more pay.

My life started to even out. And then it got better. Through friends of mine, I met a guy. Patrick lived in Fishkill and he worked in nanotechnology. He had a sailboat and we all went for a sail one day, the most fun I'd had in a long while. I felt normal for once. I felt alive. Two days later, Patrick called me for a date. For the first time in his life, he drove into Hoboken. We went out and he was polite and gentle. We took a walk in Weehawken along the river and looked over at the Manhattan skyline. He asked if he could hold my hand.

Patrick and I continued to see each other. I learned he had two sons, Eric and Kyle, from a previous marriage. He said he had married too young, and he and his wife had drifted apart. But he had an amicable relationship with her and was able to see his kids during the week and every other weekend. I'd never dated a divorced man, but Patrick seemed more mature, more focused, more certain of what he wanted in life than other men I had dated. I felt myself increasingly drawn to him.

Meanwhile, little by little, the time passed and I found myself at a point I had thought I might never reach: graduation. By some miracle, my schooling was finally over. My family all flew in for the ceremony, even Pari, who'd been in Miami. They stayed at the Hilton in Manhattan and we all had a wonderful time. I was excited to have them meet Patrick, and everyone liked him.

Two weeks later, Patrick and I went for a hike one day and he proposed. I was thrilled. Not long after that, he found us a house in upstate New York in a town called Berlin. We had talked about moving upstate and, in fact, I had been considering buying a practice in Pittsfield, Massachusetts, just over the state line. Sending out letters and resumes to practices in and around New York City had proved fruitless. Nobody was looking. My only regret in leaving New Jersey was having to say goodbye to my friends and former resident mates, Melissa and Katie. Our sisterhood was breaking up. Both would stay in New Jersey with Melissa joining her father's practice, and Katie buying a practice of her own.

The house in Berlin was beautiful, a 4,500 square-foot Victorian at the top of a hill. Patrick had to sell his condo, two sailboats, and some stock to afford it. Then he transferred his job from Fishkill to Albany. Of course, he was counting on me to help with the mortgage payment, which I was happy to do, but my negotiations for the practice in Pittsfield fell through, and I found myself without a source of income.

I went back to sending out letters and resumes, focusing now on upstate. Eventually, I spotted a classified ad—an office in Glens Falls was seeking a periodontist. I drove up there and learned that the previous periodontist had moved to Vermont but had made good money while he'd been there. I took the position, working just on Saturdays to start. Unfortunately, Patrick and I hadn't moved into our home in Berlin yet. The commute from Hoboken was four hours each way, but what choice did I have? Things became easier when we moved, but Berlin to Glens Falls was still an hour and a half.

Meanwhile, I learned of an office that needed a periodontist in Scotia, close to Schenectady. I took that position as well. I also called the doctor who had moved to Vermont and learned he needed a periodontist to help him with his work. I acquired a Vermont license and took that position too. He mentioned yet another office where a periodontist was needed in Greenville, New York. Before long, I was working out of four different offices. The position in Vermont didn't last very long once I discovered the doctor had wanted me there just to take on the cases he didn't want to handle himself, but I stuck with the other three, motivated to help with our new mortgage payment and, especially, to pay down the half a million dollars of student debt I had amassed.

The work didn't leave much free time. Finally, I decided I'd had enough driving around between three offices; I needed to open my own practice. By then, I had learned enough about New York to have fallen in love with the Hudson Valley area. Patrick had a friend in real estate who found a 1,250 square foot vacant building in Lagrangeville that had been a dentist office. The place needed a lot of updating and work, but we bought it, closing on the building in May of 2005. It was exciting to think that I would be running my own practice, and in my own building.

In the meantime, Patrick and I remained engaged, not wanting to face the prospect of having to pay for a wedding or spend the time neither one of us had to plan for one. But there was something else. I found myself hesitant to commit entirely to marrying Patrick. I loved him, there was no doubt about that, but I'd become concerned over his drinking habits. He tended to binge drink on weekends, "just to decompress," as he put it. I talked to him about the drinking, and he assured me that it wasn't a problem and, in fact, he stopped the weekend binges.

The financial considerations of a wedding were soon mitigated, too. Kia's wife Nazzi offered their home for us and promised to plan the whole thing. It was a wonderful gesture, and we accepted. We would be married after all.

Kia, by then, had been living in San Francisco, and he and Nazzi had a beautiful house. We set a date for December 17, then set a budget, which included flying out my mother, Pari, Cyrus, and Cyrus's eleven-year-old daughter, Yara. A couple of my friends—Meredith Glenn and Galina Yankulin—came, too. Patrick flew some people out, as well, including his sons and his older sister, Cathy, but of the hundred or so guests, most were local friends of Kia and Nazzi's. Still, it was a wonderful time, a traditional Persian wedding performed in both Farsi and English. We followed it up with a short, economical honeymoon in Hawaii.

In January of 2006, after months of planning and meetings with the architect and planning and zoning department, I finally opened my practice. But for the time being, in the financial situation I was in, I decided to hang on to the other positions. I felt responsible for paying my student loans on time, and also to get my co-signers off the loans as fast as possible. In fact, I added to my positions. I found two more, one in Mount Kisko and one in White Plains. With my practice in Lagrangeville, I was now working out of six locations. The house in Berlin was the farthest point from any of the offices so I soon took to sleeping in the Lagrangeville office a couple of nights a week, joining a Gold's Gym to work out, but, mostly, to make use of the shower.

The days were long and I felt as if I was on the road more than in any of the offices. I'd opened my own practice to avoid the road, but financial circumstances prevented me from taking advantage of it. I knew it was a temporary situation, that eventually I'd get caught up and would be able to work exclusively out of my own office, but in the interim, the stress began to get to me, even causing me to miss my period one month.

I mentioned it to my mom on the phone one day. "Well," she said, "there's another reason you can miss your period, you know." Truthfully, I hadn't even thought of that. On my way home that night, I stopped at a CVS and bought a pregnancy test that confirmed my mother's thoughts. I was pregnant. The news was overwhelming. I didn't feel financially secure enough to take on a pregnancy and care of an infant. But I also imagined that nobody was ever 100 percent prepared. I was happy, and so was

Patrick. Both of us imagined that parenthood could only add to the quality of our marriage.

When I had the ultrasound at five weeks, I was even more thrilled. I heard the baby's heartbeat and the idea that a human life was growing inside of me moved me greatly. At twenty weeks, I told my family. I had wanted to wait, to be sure there were no problems with the pregnancy. My baby was healthy and strong, and right on schedule for a delivery in October of 2006.

Naturally, I kept working. In fact, during this time I studied and took the exam to become board certified as a Diplomate of the American Board of Periodontology. I passed, becoming the first person in my class at UMDNJ to become a Diplomate, a proud and happy moment, a moment where my hard work and effort found some reward. Of course, Patrick and I were still in financial straits, but I savored the accomplishment, seeing it as an affirmation of my choice to have become a periodontist, and a sign that my career was moving in the right direction.

As the pregnancy continued, I gave up working in Scotia and Mamaroneck. At eight months, I took time off from all the other offices with the exception of Mount Kisko, which was right across the street from the hospital where I was going to deliver. Patrick and I also decided to downsize. The big house in Berlin, which I had fallen in love with, was not financially practical, and we both knew it. It was a dream home that we felt sure we could circle back around too later. If not that house, something similar. In the meantime, we found a much smaller house in Rhinebeck, a twenty-five-minute drive from my Lagrangeville office. The house was modest and not well constructed, but it was on a small lake. Patrick bought a rowboat immediately.

In the meantime, my mother had decided to return to Iran to sell her place there. "I'll be back before the baby is born," she promised on a phone call before she left. But I worried about her going back alone. She was seventy-four. Plus, the political situation in Iran was still unpredictable.

"Please take care of yourself," I implored.

"I'm a big girl," she said. "Don't worry. I'll be back to help with your baby boy."

"Boy?" I said. "How do you know it's going to be a boy?"

"I had a dream. And he looked just like you."

True to her word, Mom safely returned in July, planning to stay with us to help with the baby. That way, I'd be able to return to my practice. We set up the third floor for her in the Berlin house as we moved little by little into the home in Rhinebeck. One day, I packed the car full of personal belongings and drove to Rhinebeck with my mother accompanying me. Along the way, she told me of another dream.

She had seen a boy, my son, around twelve or thirteen years old. He was in a beautiful land—heaven, she said. Then she told me of still another dream. "It was of Jafar," she said. "He was telling me that you should not have this baby. And he was very sad."

Why was my mother sharing these things with me? I was nine months pregnant. I started to cry. "Why would you say something like that to me?" I said. "You are heartless!"

"And you don't appreciate me," she fired back. "You are disrespectful to your mother."

Later, I met Patrick for dinner and he could tell something was wrong. "It's nothing," I told him. "Let's just order our food. I haven't eaten all day and I'm starving."

I wouldn't have had the chance to tell him anything about my earlier conversation with Mom even if I'd wanted to. Ten minutes after we ordered, my water broke. We ran out of the restaurant, leaving the rest of the diners with their mouths hanging open.

Patrick raced me to the hospital and we checked in assuming I was soon ready to deliver. But my labor would drag on for twenty-nine hours. Until 10 p.m., September 18. But it was worth every moment. Kian was a beautiful, healthy, baby boy. I was elated; so was Patrick. The future suddenly looked brighter than it ever had before.

Chapter 5
Diagnosis

I LOVED BEING A mom. Kian became everything to me. I had no idea of the capacity for love that I had, not until Kian came along. The feelings I had for my baby were astonishing. And he was a wonderful baby, smiling and attentive.

At eight weeks, I took him to our pediatrician for a standard checkup and to get his first round of immunizations. It was a Wednesday. I wasn't looking forward to the appointment, to seeing my little guy getting stuck with a needle, but I concluded that it was all a part of motherhood and resolved that I'd be strong. Besides, I knew he wouldn't remember anything of the visit; the needle would hurt me more than Kian. I packed him into the car and my mother and I took off for the pediatrician's office for our noon appointment.

Dr. Schaffer looked Kian over and asked, "Has he just awoken from a nap?"

"No," I said. "Why do you ask?"

"Well, he seems a little low tone."

I felt my heart start to race. "What do you mean?"

Dr. Shaffer said nothing, but then lifted up Kian's arms and let them go. They fell limp to Kian's side. Then he did it again.

"What is it, doctor?" I said.

"Well, it could be botulism. Have you given him any honey by chance?"

I would learn later that botulism in infants can cause muscle weakness. And there are bacteria in honey that can cause botulism in children under twelve months.

"No," I said. "My mother gave him some rock candy with hot water to help with gas. But no honey."

"Uh-huh," he said, his brow furrowed. Then he repeated, "It could be botulism. But...there's something seriously wrong with this child. I'm going to call Westchester Medical Center and I want you to take him there. Take him there now."

Westchester Medical Center was an hour's drive away but it felt like twice that. I was in a panic, crying as I drove us there. My mother kept telling me to drive slower. "Calm down, Neda," she said. "I'm sure everything is all right."

It's what Patrick said, too, when I called him. But it was not all right. I was driving my baby to the emergency room of a hospital under the orders of a pediatrician who'd said, "There's something seriously wrong with this child." Nothing was all right.

At the hospital, the emergency room crew asked a million questions—about the birth, about my pregnancy, about Kian's diet, about everything. Then they started taking samples—blood, urine, even stool. The afternoon dragged into the evening, which dragged on into the night. By then, Patrick had finally made his way to the hospital. At nine o'clock, the ER doctor told me they were going to admit Kian to the pediatric intensive care unit and keep him until they could determine what was wrong. Patrick went home to feed the dog, while Mom and I stayed the night by Kian's bedside.

The next day, Thursday, the testing continued. Physicians and nurses came and went, including a group of resident physicians discussing Kian as if he were a case study. Finally, they scheduled a CAT scan, but the hospital was crowded and busy and we waited and waited. The morning came and went. At 2 p.m., I sought out the head doctor who brusquely said, "I have lots of sick kids here, sicker than yours. You're just going to have to sit tight." Finally, at 6 p.m., they were ready for the scan. The nurse handed me a form for permission to put Kian under general anesthetic. I said no. I didn't see any reason to put my baby under. Furthermore, I insisted I be present for the scan. After some discussion, they agreed and the scan finally commenced.

Two hours later, the head pediatrician on duty came by the room to tell us he was waiting for the radiologist's report but that he'd seen "some abnormalities with the brain." Then he turned to go.

"Abnormalities?" I said, feeling my pulse quicken. "What does that mean?"

The doctor turned back to me on his way out and replied, "It means there are things that are not normal." And then he was gone from the room and halfway down the hallway. I tried to keep my cool but it wasn't easy. I wanted to strangle the sarcasm out of that doctor, and I wondered if he had a child of his own.

The night came and went without the radiologist's report, but Friday morning, it was decided that an EMG test was in order. An electromyography test measures muscle response. It entailed sticking electrodes onto Kian's extremities and stimulating the nerve endings. I held him during the procedure and he cried the whole time. So did I.

Afterward, I asked the doctor who administered the test, "What did the test show? What's wrong with my son?"

She was writing something in a file and didn't look up at me when she answered. "There appears to be some nerve damage," she said. "Dr. Parvez, the neurologist, will explain everything to you." And then she turned and left.

For six more hours we waited. Six hours of wondering what was wrong. Finally, at 8 p.m., more than two full days after I had brought Kian to the ER, we learned what was wrong with my baby.

Spinal muscular atrophy, the number one genetic killer of infants under two, is a disease that affects one in 15,000 births in the United States. It's caused by an abnormality in a particular gene that encodes a certain protein necessary for the development and survival of motor neurons. Without these neurons, communication between the brain and skeletal muscles is impossible. Voluntary muscles become progressively weaker. SMA shows up first in the arms and legs, and then in the respiratory muscles. Infants soon cannot raise their heads and have difficulty swallowing. The later SMA appears, the milder it is. For Kian, it came early, giving him the most severe form. The typical outcome in such a case is death within months, or a couple of years at most.

Patrick and I would ultimately learn that we were both carriers of the SMA gene. One in fifty adults, in fact, is a carrier. For Patrick and me, we had a 25 percent chance of having a healthy child, 50 percent chance of having a healthy baby who would also be a carrier, and a 25 percent chance of having an affected baby.

But all of this knowledge would come later. That night, I didn't hear much beyond the fact that there was no cure and only supportive therapy was available. And then Dr. Parvez talked about Kian not making it beyond his second birthday. That's when he told me to take Kian home, take lots of pictures, and give him lots of love.

I spent the night wandering the hospital hallways. Alone. Patrick had missed all of the testing. He'd been working mostly, still under the belief that whatever was wrong, it probably wasn't that serious. I would explain it all to him later. At that point, all I could do was wander in my daze. Finally, I came across the chapel where I prayed and cried. I returned to Kian's room and held his hand and looked into his eyes. Mom was there and I could see she had been crying too. She mentioned that the doctor had come back to tell us they were going to do more blood work and send a sample to Boston to confirm the diagnosis. I clung to that word. *Confirm.* The diagnosis hadn't yet been confirmed. So maybe it was wrong.

Patrick finally returned Saturday morning and we spent the day online, learning everything we could about SMA. Mostly, we found heartbreaking photos of children suffering with the disease, with feeding tubes, and hooked up to ventilators. I finally snapped my laptop shut. I didn't want to see any more photos. In the midst of my devastation, Patrick said, "Neda, you need to let it go, you know. We need to accept what has happened." This would become a mantra for him as the days and weeks would pass, and I would wonder if it was his way of escaping emotionally from the hand we'd been dealt. To me, it seemed as if acceptance for Patrick meant pretending the circumstances didn't exist. Kian's condition couldn't hurt him if he didn't have to face it.

The blood would be drawn on Monday, so for the weekend, we were transferred to the pediatric oncology unit. Seeing the young children with cancer, their heads shaved, only added to the melancholy we felt. Monday couldn't come soon enough, but when it did, we were told to leave and come back in a few days for Kian's blood to be drawn as an outpatient. After six days and five nights, we all went home. It felt good to finally be back in my own bed. I'd lost ten pounds and was emotionally drained.

When the blood work was eventually done, the worst was, in fact, confirmed. I could no longer hang on to any hope that Kian had been somehow misdiagnosed. In my online research, I learned of a leader in the SMA field—Dr. John Bach, a professor of physical medicine and rehabilitation, as well as neurosciences, at none other than the University of Medicine and Dentistry of New Jersey. I didn't have many fond memories of my days at UMDNJ, but I was anxious to talk to him and made an appointment. Patrick, on the other hand, thought it was a waste of time. "Given Kian's condition, what is he going to be able to tell us?" he asked me. "What are you hoping to learn? All he can do is give us false hope." In the end, he agreed to come along, shrugging and saying, "Oh, well, what have we got to lose?"

Dr. Bach gave us an idea of what we were in for. "You basically have three choices as the disease progresses," he said. "First, you can do nothing. Second, you can do nothing besides having a feeding tube surgically placed through Kian's abdomen so he doesn't starve to death. Third, you can put in the tube plus bring in respiratory equipment to support his breathing so that you can prolong his life. It's all really up to you."

Patrick and I left Dr. Bach's office certain of only one thing: whatever we decided, we would never allow Kian to suffer needlessly. I became determined not to cry in front of him; I did not want Kian to sense in any way my own emotional trauma. "Patrick," I said, "We have to start living for today. It's too much to think of the future. We have to appreciate Kian right now."

Patrick nodded. "Yes," he said. "We have to forget tomorrow. After all, who knows what tomorrow is going to bring? Nobody. Nobody knows."

Chapter 6

To the Moon

WE KNEW SOMETHING ELSE besides the fact that we were not ever going to allow Kian to suffer. We knew that he deserved to live as much as anyone on earth, and it fell to us, at least in so far as it was in our power, to see to it that his life would be a quality life.

Over the next few weeks, we ordered a pulse oximeter to check Kian's oxygen level, a bipap ventilator to help with his breathing, a cough-assist machine, and a suction machine. The latter was for his saliva, knowing he would soon be unable to swallow and could choke. A respiratory therapist came out and gave us training. We also contacted the Office of Children and Family Services for an assessment. Before long, we had social workers, physical therapists, nutritionists, and an early childhood teacher come to our house to evaluate Kian's needs. If it hadn't hit us before, it certainly had by then: ours was not just a baby; ours was a special needs baby.

My mother, in the meantime, did not understand what I was feeling. Whenever I would cry, she would tell me that I should not be dwelling on Kian's condition. More than once, she told me I should not prolong his life. Spending time with him, taking pictures—it was all just going to make it harder for me. It was all going to add to the pain. "If there's a way to pull the plug," she said, "that's what I would do."

One time, I overheard her on the phone talking to somebody—probably Pari—saying, "I don't feel sorry for her. All she does is cry. And she disrespects me."

I interrupted the call. "Why would you say things like that?!" I demanded, as she hung up the phone. "Don't you see what I'm going through? How can you not feel what I am feeling?"

We argued and then she stormed out of the room, keeping to herself the rest of the day and that night. The next morning, she packed and made Patrick take her to the airport. Off she flew to Miami. I called her a few days later to check on her. Pari answered the phone and I asked to speak to Mom.

"She is not your mom," Pari sneered. Using our mother's first name, she continued, "To you, she is Azam."

"Fine," I sighed, "then let me talk to 'Azam.'"

Mom came to the phone and I asked her how she was. "I'm okay," she said coldly. Then she gave one-word answers to anything I would ask about her flight or her health. Maybe she was expecting an apology, but I was not giving her one. I had nothing to apologize for.

Finally, I said, "Well, I just wanted to know you were okay. Goodbye."

"Goodbye," she said.

My mother and I would not speak again for four years.

Patrick and I continued seeking health services for Kian, but with all the people we were in contact with, we were surprised by how few had heard of Kian's diagnosis. Even Dr. Liptay, our pediatrician, didn't know what SMA was. We soon discovered something else: our medical bills were going to be astronomical. Patrick worked for IBM at the time, and we were able to make use of his insurance. A care coordinator was assigned to the case, and she would turn out to be a godsend. DeAnna Reasor Weekes was an RN by trade and had a wonderful understanding of what we needed, often fighting with the insurance company on our behalf.

But even with the insurance, I knew there were going to be heavy financial demands ahead of us. And I still had my student loans to pay off and the building loan for my new practice, over a million dollars combined. Eventually, the student loan deferrals came to an end and I scraped to make the minimum monthly payments. I went back to working in the Lagrangeville, Glens Falls, Greenville, Mount Kisko, and White Plains offices, living mostly out of the car, leaving Kian in the care of nurses. The stress was nearly unbearable. I lost weight. My hair started falling out. In the offices, I put on a smile and never talked about my personal life. Nobody knew my situation but, in the car, driving to and from, I would often cry until there were no more tears to shed.

And of course I cried for Kian. I still had so many questions about the disease. To get a better handle on what I could expect in taking care of an SMA baby, DeAnna put me in touch with a woman who had two of them. Sue lived in Vermont and over the phone, she told me of her two boys and what was in store for me.

"You'll get used to most things," Sue told me, "but the episodes will always be difficult."

"Episodes?" I asked. "What do you mean?"

"When they stop breathing. Their oxygen will nosedive. You'll know it when it happens."

In time, I would learn how right she was.

On a Monday in March of 2007, I noticed Kian didn't seem to be himself. He spent most of the morning fussing. Around noon, I took his temperature and it was 103. I called Dr. Liptay who told us to bring him in. Patrick and I drove to her office where she examined Kian, and, with a very concerned expression, said, "He's congested and his lungs aren't clear. He may be developing pneumonia. Now, normally I would send you to the hospital for a chest X-ray, but in this case, well, we know how bad Kian's prognosis is. It's up to you what you want to do with him. I'm going to give you a prescription for antibiotics. Take him home and call me tomorrow. Hopefully, the antibiotics will get the fever down. If not, you can always take him to the hospital."

I thanked her on our way out, and she said, "I'm very sorry about your son."

Out in the hallway, I broke down, telling Patrick through my tears that I was never going be able to get used to this. Was every fever going to portend the last days of Kian's life?

The next day, with the fever unabating, I took Kian to Vassar Brothers Medical Center where they did a chest X-ray. Kian, thankfully, did not have pneumonia. Instead, he had bronchitis and the doctor wanted to keep him for a few days, putting him on IV antibiotics. While Kian was in the hospital, I still had to work. The bills and student loans were not going away. But I couldn't stand the thought of Kian all alone in the hospital, with just the nurses coming and going from his room and nobody to sit with him. And what if he had an episode when nobody was around? We had a babysitter named Dana and I hired her to spend the days with Kian. Then I came in each evening to spend all night with him. At times, I couldn't help but wonder how much easier it would have been if I'd had family in town, but of course my mother and siblings were all living elsewhere.

Kian got past the bronchitis, but then came the issue of his feeding. The long-term solution was a gastric tube. This is what Dr. Bach had mentioned, a tube that would be inserted directly into Kian's abdomen. For the time being, he was being fed with a nasogastric tube. An NG tube is a catheter that runs through the nose and down into the stomach. Vassar didn't have pediatric surgeons to perform the insertion of the gastric tube, and I soon learned that the only place willing to do the surgery with local anesthetic was the UMDNJ University Hospital in Newark. Local anesthesia was imperative. I worried otherwise that the surgery would be too much for Kian, that it would weaken him to where he would not be able to breathe on his own. I knew that was coming anyway, but I didn't see any reason to speed the process up.

Patrick thought we shouldn't do the surgery at all, or to do only what the doctors would recommend. It was the first indication that he and I were not seeing eye to eye on our future course of action. "Neda," he said, "are we doing the right things? Maybe by prolonging his life, we're only prolonging his suffering."

"Well, I disagree," I said. "I'm not giving up on this boy. We need to do whatever it takes. If I have to fly him to the moon, I'll find a way."

The problem with UMDNJ was that it was not under our insurance plan. The company would cover neither the transport nor the surgery. With DeAnna's help, I fought with them and finally they acquiesced and agreed to cover the expenses. Kian and I took an ambulance ride to UMD-NJ, a place I never thought I'd be happy to return to, but I was happy that day. I knew that there were doctors there who understood SMA and who could help my child.

The surgery was successful. But now I recognized that we were going to need twenty-four-hour nursing care. Kian's condition was making him progressively more fragile. Clearly, a nurse needed to be present at all times. I fought with the insurance company again. Initially, they denied the coverage, saying that Kian needed not nursing care, but hospice care. My appeal was denied. Then I set about gathering letters from the doctors at UMDNJ stating that Kian was not necessarily terminal. Hospice care was not appropriate. We needed nurses. Again, they denied the care that we needed, and again I appealed. This time, the nursing care was approved.

This was a lesson in tenacity that would serve me well going forward. Later, I would learn from other mothers of disabled children that forty hours per week of nursing care is almost always the maximum allowed.

Getting caught in our broken healthcare system and being at the mercy of the insurance companies was illuminating. What I'd learned about our system in my years of schooling, and the time I'd spent observing it from the perspective of my professional practice, was all theoretical. But it wasn't just theory for me now. From the patient's perspective, fighting for my child's life, I was getting a *real* education.

Meanwhile, Patrick and I continued disagreeing about Kian's treatment. I suppose everyone handles these things in their own way. Patrick's way was to lean into his newfound Buddhist beliefs. Kian was "enlightened," he would tell me. Kian had "reached a higher state" than all of us. Then he would tell me that I needed to let it go, that I was dwelling too much on Kian's suffering. But I knew what he really meant. For Patrick, letting "it" go meant letting Kian go.

At one point, Patrick went to a workshop led by Robert Schwartz, author of a book called *Courageous*

Souls. Schwartz believed, and preached, that souls choose their eternal paths, meaning they choose whom to be born as. Kian, according to this theory, chose his lot in life before he was born. Further, he chose what family to be born into, presumably choosing us as his parents. Patrick came home from the workshop with a signed copy of Schwartz's book, which I read to appease him. And then I promptly tore the cover off the book in anger, throwing the book across the room. *Who would choose any of this?*

In the meantime, I had read a book of my own. *God's Problem* by Bart Ehrman dealt with the question of why an all-powerful God would permit suffering. The idea didn't make sense in Ehrman's view. If there's a God, it cannot be an active, loving God. For the first time in my life, I began to doubt God's existence. Kian's condition made no sense to me, and consequently, neither did the idea of a God that would allow it. I was slowly becoming an atheist. Patrick and I weren't disagreeing just on Kian's course of care; our worldviews were clashing. And I was feeling increasingly alone.

As the days and weeks and then months wore on, I found myself in a depression. I cried a lot. I held Kian. Patrick and the nurses and I played with him as best we could, bringing him toys that he could not himself play with. We would read to him or sing to him. I wrote to the

SMA Foundation for information one time, and they sent us a care package that included a little red wagon. Many mornings, I would transfer Kian into the wagon and we would take him for walks around the neighborhood. His eyes would brighten at the outside world around him. The wagon was the only spot I could make Kian comfortable that wasn't a bed, and I hated the idea of keeping my son in a bed all day.

But then I would have to go to work. Always, I had to go to work. And I would think of how I was able to walk around on my own two working legs, how I could grab hold of an item with my hands, how I could eat, how I could do all the things people take for granted, and how Kian could do none of those things. Worse, I would see the babies of other mothers, raising their hands and kicking their feet, their bodies responding to their brains, even if just subconsciously. Kian's body had failed him. If I could have traded places with him, I would have.

I knew I needed to talk to someone. I could not accept what was happening to my son. I thought about a therapist, but then decided on somebody else. Stacey Wolfe was a famous New York City author and psychic. I'd heard her on the radio before and I liked her. Maybe it was an act of desperation, but despite my growing sense that the universe was a cold, godless, unfathomable place, I had a feeling that Stacey would be able to help me in some way.

I made an appointment, told her something of my situation, and listened as she gave me the best advice I would ever receive. "Neda," she said, "you have to stop beating yourself. You have to stop feeling sorry for yourself and for Kian. It's not helping either of you. Your son needs love. Your son needs a mom. You must stop saying, 'Why me?' and 'Why him?' You need to enjoy being a mom."

Enjoy being a mom. The idea had not even remotely occurred to me, and I was immediately overcome by emotion. Was I allowed to "enjoy" being the mother of an SMA baby? Could a person really do that? It was as if I had needed permission and Stacey was giving it to me. And then she told me something else: "Your son is going to survive into his teens," she said. "You'll have a lot of time to spend with him."

I left Stacey Wolfe's office feeling completely changed. My perspective swung 180 degrees. Yes, I was the mother of an SMA baby, but I was more than this. I was a *mom*, and I needed to live and act like a mom, like the mom that Kian deserved, for whatever amount of time he would be with us. And like the mom that, deep down, I knew I really wanted to be.

I continued seeking practical help, eventually finding a group of SMA moms online. But quickly I was able to gather that, though no doubt well-intentioned, the group was something of a place for stay-at-home moms to go to seek sympathy, bordering at times, it seemed to me, on being one, big online pity party. I didn't need sympathy. I wasn't looking for shoulders to cry on. I wanted constructive, useable advice, and I found it in another SMA mom named Deborah Heine.

Deborah and her husband Chris started the Claire Altman Heine Foundation, named after their SMA daughter. Claire passed away at nine months. Through their foundation, Deborah and Chris were lobbying for a national health policy to promote testing for SMA for couples thinking of having a baby. I came across their website and called Deborah, looking for whatever helpful information she could pass along to me. She was happy to talk. At one point, she was in New York City on a business trip and I hopped on a train to meet her. We had coffee and she told me that she and Chris had decided at the time of Claire's diagnosis to sign a do not resuscitate order. They had essentially let Claire pass away. But she was quick to tell me that whatever path I chose, it had to be the right one for me. There was no right or wrong for decisions of such magnitude. Neither way makes you a good parent or a bad parent.

She was also quick to warn me that doctors like Dr. Bach, whom she had also consulted, were always going to make you feel as if you should do everything in your power to keep your child alive, as if there's hope for some kind of better quality of life. "But there's not," Deborah told me. "This is a very sad, degenerative disease that will never get better."

Nor does the grief when your baby dies, she told me. "We've got two other children, but not a day goes by that I don't think about Claire," she said. "You never get over it. It stays with you always. In fact, we couldn't bring ourselves to bury Claire, to say goodbye to her. We had her cremated and when I die, her ashes will be buried with me."

I cried on the train ride home. And I thought about the DNR that Deborah had mentioned. I was fully committed to keeping Kian alive, but at what cost? What would the emergency technicians do if Patrick and I were not home and the nurse had called 911 because Kian had stopped breathing? How far would they go without a DNR in place? The thought of losing Kian suddenly took a backseat to the idea of Kian suffering.

I talked it over with Patrick when I got home, but, of course, I knew he was already in favor of a DNR. I was the one who'd rebuffed the idea. But now I was ready to protect Kian from needless suffering, even if it meant his life. We made an appointment with the nurse manager at Northern Dutchess Hospital in Rhinebeck to sign a DNR, but after hearing the list of all the potential scenarios and having to agree to withhold treatment for each one, to basically allow Kian to die, I found myself hesitating. Deborah's baby had contracted pneumonia and she had withheld antibiotics. Claire died not long afterward in Deborah's arms, eventually running out of breath. Oxygen was also withheld. Deborah was absolutely correct that there was no right or wrong to such a heartrending decision. I would never in a million years second-guess any parent's course of action in such painful circumstances. Nobody has the right to judge anyone else's choice. I could only do what I thought was right for Kian and me. I told Patrick I could not sign the DNR.

We drove home with me feeling relieved. But then we argued about it. Patrick felt a DNR was in Kian's "best interest." I lost my temper. "I hope something happens to you someday that will leave you defenseless!" I said. "Then you'll get a taste of your own selfishness!" It was said in the heat of the moment, but in my mind the accusation of selfishness was wholly accurate. For Patrick, I knew that "best interest" was a rationalization and a DNR gave him a way to assuage any feelings of guilt or responsibility. His desire for a DNR was not the desire of a caring parent like Deborah. Patrick wanted to be free of Kian.

This was a growing sense I'd had about Patrick. At first, I tried to deny it. Surely, he was a good man and a loving father. But I could not ignore his behavior. He resented the circumstances we'd been presented with. Not for Kian's sake, but for his own. He'd started drinking more. The weekend binges had begun again. Patrick wanted to escape from Kian. He planned trips to Europe for us, as if we could just get away anytime we wanted. He spent time in Syracuse with his sister Cathy.

Patrick seemed to be moving on from Kian. I was going in the opposite direction. There would be no DNR. I had made my choice, and it didn't matter to me that Patrick was not on board, nor my mother, nor any doctor. Ahead of me was being the best mom I could be to Kian, for as long as I could be.

Chapter 7

The First Year

KNOWING I COULD NOT agree to the DNR, I doubled down on the idea of being the best mother I could be. I could not allow Kian to simply pass away. I would do whatever it took to help him live, so long as he was not suffering. When, at last, I would inevitably lose him, I never wanted to have to think that I could have done more. I knew I wouldn't be able to live with that. And now, with Stacey Wolfe's advice still clear in my mind, I was not going to show Kian my own suffering. I would not cry in front of him, and I would not allow him to sense my anxiety. I would smile for him instead, and be a calming, loving presence. I would enjoy being a mom.

I also decided to start taking better care of myself. I knew I had let my own health slide, but I needed to stay well for Kian. I hit the gym and started running again. I sought acupuncture care. I went back to eating healthy foods and made a determination to nourish my body and mind.

If I couldn't get any emotional support from my own mother, I could at least get it from other family members. Kia was a constant source of encouragement. He would call from San Francisco and tell me, "Don't worry about Mom. She doesn't understand. She doesn't have the education or upbringing that you have. You're doing all the right things, Neda. Kian knows it. He's a smart little boy. And you're going to have other kids and they'll get to know Kian and they'll see what a great mom you are."

The idea of having more children was something Patrick and I talked about. I wanted more kids, even as the marriage seemed increasingly unstable. Patrick would have been done with children, but he knew how strongly I felt. We didn't want to take any chances, however. SMA is genetic. The risk was small, but the risk had been small with Kian. Both of us agreed that embryo testing would be imperative.

It didn't take long before I experienced one of the episodes that Sue from Vermont had warned me about. One morning, I left the house for a haircut, leaving Tiffany, one of the agency nurses with Kian. As my hair was being rinsed, my cell phone rang. It was Tiffany. "Kian is okay," she said, her voice shaking slightly, "but he's on his way to Vassar Brothers hospital."

"The hospital? What happened?" I asked.

"He was having an awful time breathing."

I paid my bill, put my wet hair in a ponytail, jumped in my car, and sped off for the hospital, calling Vassar's ER along the way. The staff said that Kian had been transported to Northern Dutchess hospital in Rhinebeck. I made a U-turn and started driving for Northern Dutchess, arriving fifteen minutes later where I was greeted by Kathy, the supervising nurse.

"Your son is okay," she said. "He's been intubated."

We'd never wanted Kian to be intubated. Putting a tube down a person's trachea to supply oxygen comes with risks in the best of scenarios. Dr. Bach had warned us that for an SMA baby, the risks are much greater, including the risk of infection and lung complications. This, after all, was what the bipap machine was for. I explained this to Kathy, trying to keep myself from exploding.

"We would have lost him otherwise," she said.

We made our way to where Kian was. He was now stable and resting, but I winced at the sight of him with the tube. I told Kathy I'd like to speak to the EMS people who had brought Kian in. She left and a few minutes later, Joe and Tony, the two guys who had responded to Tiffany's 911 call, came into the room. I closed the door and asked them what had happened.

"Well," said Joe, "we saw that your son was having difficulty breathing, even with the bipap machine. His heart rate was up and he looked like he had no muscle tone."

Of course he had no muscle tone. "Did Tiffany, the nurse, tell you he's an SMA baby?" I asked.

"No, ma'am," Joe replied. "I don't know what an SMA baby is."

"Did she tell you anything about his medical history?"

"No, ma'am."

Tiffany had obviously panicked. She allowed the EMS technicians to take control without briefing them on the situation to give them all the facts they needed to make the right assessment. It would be an early sign that the nursing agency might not be up to the task.

I called Patrick, but kept getting his voicemail, leaving him messages about where Kian and I were. Then I decided to have Kian transferred to UMDNJ where I trusted the staff. I called the attending physician who told me not to allow Northern Dutchess to extubate Kian. "If the baby goes into respiratory distress, he's better off here."

Patrick finally called back and met me at Northern Dutchess just before the ambulance was ready to transport Kian.

"Why don't you just have them take the tube out here?" he asked. "And then put on the bipap. Neda, this seems kind of like a waste of time."

"The doctor at UMDNJ told me we should wait until we get there."

"Of course he did! They want the insurance money."

Patrick in my mind had forfeited his advocacy for Kian. I didn't need his opinion or his approval. "I don't care," I told him. "I'd feel a lot more comfortable at UMDNJ, so that's where we're going, and we're going to let them extubate him."

Patrick shook his head as I got into the ambulance with Kian. It was another moment where I felt all alone. But I didn't have time to feel sorry for myself. I looked over at my son and knew that I was doing the right thing, the thing that was best for him.

At the New Jersey state line, we were told we could go no farther. We had just come off of three days of heavy rain. Seven inches had fallen around the greater New Jersey area and the streets we needed to access were flooded. Kian, still determined to be in physical danger, would need to be taken by helicopter instead. The ambulance drove to a field in Mahwah where Kian was transferred to a waiting helicopter in which there was no room for me. I hated to be separated from him, but I knew it was the only way.

After the chopper took off, I ended up being driven to the hospital by a state trooper who took several detours to avoid the flooded areas.

Kian was extubated the next day and responded well. The day after that, we were able to check out of the hospital. But I was left with an even clearer idea of all that we were going to have to face. "The episodes will always be difficult," Sue had said. She wasn't kidding.

To make matters worse, Patrick had come to pick us up from the hospital but hadn't bothered to notice the car was low on gas. Halfway home, we sputtered to a stop on the side of the Garden State Parkway. Patrick had to walk two miles to a gas station while I remained in the car with Kian, wondering what I could possibly do if we had another emergency right then and there. How would I save him? I held Kian in my arms and prayed to a God I wasn't sure existed. Patrick made it back with a can of gas and we were able to get on our way, but I was left wondering even more about the capabilities of the man I had married.

Back home, we strove for normalcy. I doted on Kian as much as I could, given the constraints of my work schedule. Yes, he was a special needs baby, but that didn't mean we couldn't treat him like other toddlers. Besides the walks, we traveled with him. We went to Baltimore once for a long weekend. I had a certification class I needed to take in Charleston. South Carolina, so we took him to Charleston. I fell in love with the city, with the charm of its historic buildings and the cobblestone streets where I strolled with Kian. On the way back, I promised myself I'd return and walk those streets again someday.

For Kian's first birthday, a birthday we had not even been assured of, we had a party. DeAnna, our care coordinator, came and I was able to meet her face-to-face for the first time. She brought Kian a soft blanket that I have to this day, and a CD of the Beatles with "Here Comes the Sun," which quickly became our song. The party was bittersweet. We all sang "Happy Birthday" and we opened gifts, but Kian could not sit, he could not roll, he could not move, and he could not eat the birthday cake we'd bought for the occasion, though I let him taste the icing. But he was still able to smile, and he did so, his eyes lighting up at the attention. He cooed and seemed genuinely happy. I wanted to cry but willed myself not to.

Somehow, we had made it through a year. It had been a long one. I had no idea what the second year of Kian's life would bring, but I was beginning to have serious doubts about the nursing agency. It was clear that some nurses were better than others, and we were never given a choice. We were stuck with the agency the insurance company had selected and even though DeAnna was constantly working to make sure we were getting everything we needed, the staff often disappointed us. There seemed to be a revolving door of nurses and, in fact, over the first two years, we would have a total of forty-two nurses come into our home to take care of Kian.

My trust issues started with the first episode, when Tiffany had failed to brief the EMS techs about Kian's condition. From then on, I found it difficult for me to leave Kian alone all day with a nurse while Patrick and I went to work. I could never seem to relax when I was away from home. It didn't help that I'd sometimes have to take calls from the nurses telling me that Kian was having a tough day. Finally, my office manager suggested we clean out some space and bring Kian in. I thought it was a wonderful idea and from then on, I brought Kian to work with me, along with all his equipment and the nurse.

But one afternoon, not long after we started doing this, Kian had another episode. He stopped breathing. I heard the panic-stricken nurse shouting my name and I dropped what I was doing and ran into where Kian was. The nurse froze and I found myself resuscitating my son without her help, using heavy suctioning to start, and then mouth-to-mouth. Kian came around and was soon his normal self, and I saw no reason to take him to the hospital and risk intubation. These episodes, I now realized, were simply going to be part of our lives, part of the day-to-day challenges we were going to face. Still, I was shaken and I knew I could not continue to work that day. I had the nurse drive us home with me in the backseat with Kian in case I needed to resuscitate him again. When we arrived, I told the nurse to leave. Patrick came home and when I recounted what had happened, how the nurse had frozen, he called the agency and screamed at them.

This was shortly followed by another disturbing incident. Another nurse, one that I had hired on my own, witnessed one of the agency's nurses manhandling Kian roughly enough to cause him to cry in pain. Patrick surreptitiously set up a video camera the next day and we were able to see this nurse's harsh way of handling our son. It was heartbreaking and infuriating. We brought it to the attention of the agency and instead of addressing the problem with their nurse, they objected to the video camera. "None of our nurses want to lose their licenses," one of the directors at the agency told us. Coming on the heels of the episode in my office, not to mention the earlier episode with Tiffany, it was plain even to the agency that they were out of their league. Their nurses were not trained to manage an SMA child. Before long, they made the decision to drop us as clients.

I protested to DeAnna, but there was nothing she could do. Worse, this was the only agency in the area at the time. On the other hand, their level of care had been far less than what Kian required, so I wondered if maybe it was a blessing in disguise. But how would I replace them? Even a less than ideal nurse was better than no nurse at all.

Until I could figure something out, the nurse I had hired on my own—Debra Duryea—agreed to come in every day. It was a huge help to have the same nurse there, one who came to understand the needs of Kian, and one with whom Kian was obviously comfortable. They'd become close in a short time. But I knew that one nurse would never be enough.

"What are we going to do?" I asked DeAnna.

"Well, you hired one nurse on your own, right?"

"Yes. And basically trained her."

"So hire another one. And train her. Put it through the same billing company that Debra works out of. I'll make sure IBM approves it."

Without knowing it, or certainly planning for it, I was, for all intents and purposes, about to start my own nursing agency. If I couldn't find an agency that was satisfactory, I would build one instead, full of nurses with sufficient knowledge of the requirements of an SMA baby.

Chapter 8

Seeking Hope

I BEGAN HIRING NURSES and training them. I outsourced the billing to the same billing company that was paying Debra, a small company run by a man in the Bronx named Ralph. But one day, Debra came to me and told me the electric company had cut off her power.

"Ralph's not paying me," she said. "He keeps telling me the insurance company is delaying their payments." I called the power company on Debra's behalf, paying her overdue bill with my credit card, but it was a weekend and her power wouldn't be turned on again until Monday. I sent Patrick to Home Depot to buy a generator that he took to Debra's house. Then I called DeAnna and asked for advice on dealing with the billing company.

"Well, you could always start doing your own billing," she suggested. I liked the idea, knowing it would give me more control. I didn't like the fact that some guy named Ralph in the Bronx was in charge of paying my nurses. But to be acceptable to the insurance company, I needed legitimacy. And so I set up a company, calling it Advanced Medical Billing and Staffing. At the same time, I started the seven-year process to obtain a New York State license for a full-blown nursing agency, an agency dedicated to the skilled nursing care of children like Kian with rare conditions. I would handpick the nurses, and the agency would have far more trained nurses than any other agency in the entire upstate region. I'd also offer nutritional support care, which would require another permit, this one taking a decade to obtain.

The nursing agency would be called Millennium Children's Homecare, but Advance Medical Billing would provide a bridge to Kian's care in the interim. To my pleasant surprise, the New York State Health Department approved my plan. Soon, I was assigned folks in the department who were fully aware of Kian's struggles. Before long, I was running a fully staffed company, hiring superstar nurses, training them, scheduling them, paying them, and directly billing the insurance company. Plus, working at multiple periodontal office locations.

Through it all, I had to be the best periodontist I could be for my patients. I had to remain informed on industry developments and stay up to date with the latest technology. I had to wine and dine my referring doctors, too, and I made sure never to talk about my family life. I feared that if they knew what I was dealing with, they'd stop giving me work. I never confided in patients or assistants, either, always saying everything was great if they asked about Kian. I couldn't afford to appear to anyone as if I were struggling. I couldn't jeopardize my means of making a living. Now, besides all the other bills, I had nurses to pay, and I made a determination that their payments would never be late. Even if I had to fight with the insurance company later, my nurses wouldn't have to wait, wouldn't have to worry any longer about paying their electric bills. The nurses became the top priority.

I felt at times that I was living a double life. On the surface, everything was great but the reality was that I was working to pay student loans, the nurses, and everything else. There was no room to show any sign of weakness or struggles. My life was about Kian, and whatever needed to be done to keep him safe and comfortable.

I got only a few hours' sleep each night, but I kept going. I kept working. I knew I had to be strong for Kian. Often, I would think back to my father. Life had defeated him. I would not allow life to defeat me.

In the midst of all this, Patrick and I were trying for another baby. Kian had been conceived on our first try but now weeks and months were going by and I was unable to get pregnant again. My OBGYN suggested that the problem was the pressure I was under. The stress was having an effect on my reproductive system. She told me that Patrick and I would need to try unsuccessfully for a full year before a conclusion could be drawn that there was a fertility problem.

Patrick agreed, believing that if I were in a more relaxed state, we wouldn't be having any issues, but I went for a second opinion from another OBGYN, a young Iranian doctor nearby who was happy to refer us to a fertility center in Albany where I explained our SMA concerns. We decided to do intrauterine insemination. They prescribed fertility drugs to increase the odds of conception, injections that I was able to give myself. This wasn't easy. I was used to giving people injections in their mouths, but now that I had to give myself injections, it was a different story.

The day we had the insemination done I started thinking about what would happen if the pregnancy occurred but the testing showed an SMA baby. How would I feel about terminating the pregnancy? In theory, it seemed the only rational choice, but would I think differently in the actual moment of decision? Two weeks later, I had my period and found myself feeling relieved.

After that, we decided on in vitro fertilization, where the embryo could be tested prior to implantation, but soon it was determined that my FSH hormone was elevated, a symptom, perhaps, of premature ovarian failure. I would be tested periodically, but for the time being, the IVF was postponed and I was taken off the fertility drugs. We went back to the inseminations, despite my apprehensions, but got nowhere. Out and about, I would see pregnant women, or women with babies, and I couldn't help feeling envious. What a difference a year had made. It wasn't long ago, I thought, that I was pregnant with Kian—happy, excited, looking forward to his arrival and the start of a new life for Patrick and me. How everything had changed.

My efforts to become pregnant dragged on for months. With constant appointments and testing, it became like another job, as if I needed one. One night at dinner, I told Patrick that I was no longer going to worry about becoming pregnant. "I'm going to enjoy Kian as long as possible," I said. "As long as he's here. And when he's gone, that will be it."

"What do you mean?"

"I mean when he goes, I'll go."

"What? Neda, you're scaring me."

"Well, I'm happy with Kian. Being his mom is everything to me. I don't want to face a world with him not in it. I only want to be his mom."

For all the trouble, I *was* happy with Kian, no matter the day-to-day difficulties, nor the all-out emergencies. As Kian grew, I never forgot Stacey Wolfe's advice: *You need to enjoy being a mom.* Yes, I worked incessantly, but I tried my best each day to be home before dark. Often, I spent the night with Kian. He was on his own schedule and he seemed to prefer staying up most of the night and sleeping in late, which was perfect for me. "Are we pulling an all-nighter?" I would ask, and he would coo to me. Then we'd watch movies together or reruns of *American Idol*. I would suction his saliva and sometimes give him some ice cream or candy. Often, I would massage him, loosening whatever knots he might have in his little arms and legs. Those nights were special to me. They were special for both of us.

Our weekends were special, too. With Kian, I could escape the hustle and bustle of everyday life. My time with him allowed me to see and experience what's really important. My true priorities came into focus. I'd push him around the neighborhood in a stroller. My dental assistant had a farm and one time she brought me four chicks to take home for the weekend. I placed them one by one into Kian's hand, then took his other hand and helped him pet them. He smiled up at me. Later, he would lose the ability to smile, but I would never forget his happy face.

But of course the life-threatening dangers of SMA never went away. It didn't help to know that SMA was so little understood, even within the medical community. One morning, Kian had a raspy sound in his left lung and Patrick took him to Children's Medical Group. I was in my office in the midst of an incredibly involved case, placing six implants in a patient who'd lost all his teeth. A rep from the implant company had even come into town to observe the surgery. It was the biggest case I'd ever done. Patrick called right before the surgery to tell me that the staff at Children's had called for an ambulance and Kian was headed for Westchester Medical Center.

I had my responsibilities to my patient. There was nobody to turn the surgery over to. It was one of the longest days of my life, but finally, by 6 p.m., I was headed for the hospital to see my son. When I arrived, the attending physician said that Kian was doing fine, but that they wanted to keep him overnight for observation. They were preparing to transfer him out of the ER and into the pediatric intensive care ward. We stayed with Kian until a nurse came to make the transfer. I asked for a cough machine.

"Oh, we don't have one of those," she said, "but we really don't need it."

"Yes, you do," I protested. "When you take the ventilator off of him, you're going to need to use the cough machine; otherwise his oxygen saturation will go down." This was just one of the many things I had had to learn over the past year, the things I had even taught my nurses. I knew Kian. I knew SMA.

"We know what we're doing, Mom," the nurse said, breezily waving aside my concerns. Sure enough, by the time Kian made it to the pediatric intensive care floor, his oxygen was dangerously low. He was full of saliva. Worse, their suction unit was not working properly. Kian couldn't breathe. In front of us, he coded. I rushed toward him, wanting to resuscitate him myself, something I had become expert at, but a doctor held me back. All I could do was watch as they intubated him, the very thing we were trying to avoid. I was stunned by how little the hospital staff seemed to understand Kian's condition, and how unprepared they were.

Two days later, Kian was home again, but that just meant we were between life-threatening crises. When would the next one come? I tried to live in the moment, appreciating my time with Kian, but I yearned for a long-term solution. One night, I was watching NBC Nightly News with Brian Williams and a report came on about a little girl with glycogen storage disease, a rare metabolic disorder that had relegated her to a wheelchair. Her parents managed to raise enough money from the people in their town to fly her to China for stem cell treatment. Three months later, the little girl was walking. It was nothing less than a miracle, and even though I'd stopped believing in miracles, I knew I had to learn more about this amazing treatment.

Stem cells are the most fundamental cells in the human body, the cells from which all other cells are made. Stem cell therapy is a way to generate healthy cells to replace diseased cells. But it is not without its controversies. Although adult stem cells can be used, embryonic stem cells show much more promise, but this brings up ethical concerns about the use of embryos. And the effectiveness of stem cell therapy is far from assured. Clinical trials continue, but the FDA has not approved stem cell products for general use. Hence, the desire of the little girl's parents to go to China.

I scoured the internet for all that I could find about stem cell procedures. I researched the NBC story and found the hospital that did the treatment. It was in Hangzhou, in the Zhejiang province. But in doing further research, I could find no cases of stem cell treatment for babies or for anybody with SMA. Was the treatment inappropriate for Kian's case? I contacted the hospital and talked to a treatment plan coordinator who spoke very optimistically. For the first time since Kian's diagnosis, I felt hope. The procedure was $20,000 and they needed a $4,000 deposit. I wired it to them the next day.

Then I went looking for the balance. We simply didn't have it. I contacted several charitable organizations seeking financial help, organizations that raised money for children in need, but nobody was willing to help fund what was considered to be "experimental" medical treatment, especially from China. It was disheartening. I mentioned our dilemma to Janine, one of the dental assistants in the Glens Falls office and she said that her husband, who was a member of the Glens Falls fire department might be able to help. They frequently hosted benefit events at the firehouse, she told me.

But in the meantime, I was having second thoughts about China. They were emailing information on the procedure and mentioned in one email that we needed to bring our own gloves if we wanted them. The hospital didn't have gloves? Needless to say, this was disconcerting. When I emailed about Kian's oxygen requirements and the need for a suction machine, I received an email back saying they were very sorry, but it seemed as though Kian was "medically unstable," and therefore could not be admitted to their program.

I would have been heartbroken, except for the reservations I was having about the Hangzhou hospital. Like with the nursing agency dumping us, maybe this too was a blessing. And I knew there had to be other stem cell treatment providers somewhere. I jumped back on the computer, eventually finding International BioCare in Tijuana, Mexico.

I had a much better feeling about BioCare. The doctors were skilled Americans who regularly traveled to Tijuana to do stem cell treatments. They could treat Kian on an out-patient basis. The cost was $25,000, but now our transportation expenses would be lower. We just needed to get to San Diego and they would send a van for us from there.

But there was still the matter of the money. I got the runaround from the hospital in Hangzhou about returning my deposit until I eventually threatened to take my complaint to the media, knowing they received a lot of their business from the US and could not afford the bad publicity. Two days later, the $4,000 was wired back to me.

After hearing our story, the firehouse did, indeed, hold a benefit for Kian, a spaghetti dinner. I registered a "Baby Kian" fund with the IRS and did a mass mailing to everyone I knew asking for donations. All told, we raised $11,000. It was a lot, but it wasn't enough. With no other options, I took on yet one more job, this one at a four-location periodontist practice in Rochester, a three-hour drive away. After six months, I was able to save enough for the trip and treatment.

Of course, a big question was how best to get to San Diego. A commercial flight would be out of the question. What if Kian had an event mid-air? Naturally, this would have been an even bigger problem had we been able to go to China, another reason I was happy to have found an alternative. I contacted Angel Flight, a non-profit organization that provides free air transportation for people with medical needs, but the farthest they flew was 300 miles. I called around to get rental rates on an RV, and then finally decided on train transportation. Lorna, one of our nurses, offered to go along, which was a tremendous help.

We took the train from Albany to Chicago, and, after an eight-hour layover, took another train to Los Angeles, and then to San Diego. From there we were picked up by the hospital van and driven across the border to Tijuana. The procedure included an injection into Kian's spine, and then there was nothing more to do but go home and wait. The doctor cautioned us not to expect to see any results right away, but days went by, and then weeks, and then months. I knew all along—during all of the internet research, the planning, the fundraising, the extra hours of work, the long train ride across the country—that nothing was guaranteed. It had always been a gamble. Still, it was impossible to push aside the feelings of defeat and down-heartedness as time went on, and our hopes for any kind of recovery for Kian slowly faded away.

Chapter 9
Joys and Sorrows

WE NEEDED A VICTORY, a reason for celebration, and the end of 2007 brought a Christmas miracle. Without intrauterine insemination, without in vitro fertilization, without fertility shots, I somehow became pregnant. A blood test a few days after Christmas confirmed a home pregnancy test I had taken on Christmas Eve. More good news followed: a chorionic villus sampling—a prenatal test of the fetus for chromosomal disorders and genetic abnormalities—showed nothing. My baby was not going to be an SMA baby. And, in fact, my baby was going to be another boy. I was elated.

At the time, I was still working in Rochester a couple days a week. I'd leave the house every Sunday afternoon for the six-hour drive and check into a Rochester hotel where I'd stay. Driving in the winter in that part of the country was not ideal. Sometimes, it could be downright dicey. More than once, I faced brief periods of whiteout conditions, making the trip twice as long and twice as nerve-wracking. In April, I decided to stop working in Rochester. I was now on the road a lot less, but I was still splitting my time between multiple offices.

During the course of the pregnancy, Kian had several episodes. I started to worry about leaving him alone when the time would come for me to deliver. My work schedule was predictable and I could plan ahead, making sure the nurses were in place but labor could come at any time. What if I had to be rushed to the hospital in the middle of the night? I decided I needed to plan the birth. At thirty-five weeks, I asked to be induced and my doctor agreed. On August 13, 2008, Debra came to the house at 7 a.m., and Patrick and I drove to the hospital. Everything was on schedule. But soon after I was induced, I had an adverse reaction to the medication I'd been given and my blood pressure dropped to a dangerously low 80/40. They rushed me into the operating room for an emergency C-section. It was terrifying. "Please don't let my baby die," I cried to the doctors. But at 3:30 p.m., my beautiful baby was born, second in beauty only to his older brother Kian. We named him Kamran.

Although the hospital staff insisted I stay for three days of observation, I signed myself out the next day. I had to get home to Kian. Sitting around for observation wasn't a part of the plan. Two weeks later, despite the fact that I'd just had a C-section, I was back at work. Money continued to be a problem. My bills didn't stop and I was still just barely making the minimum payments on my student loans. And now, with Kami, I needed to arrange for childcare in addition to Kian's nurses.

But things felt different now. Bringing Kami home was like filling the house with sunshine. In no time, he was holding his head up and meeting all the early milestones. Kami looked just like me. Same brown eyes, same brown hair. If you would have put his picture next to my baby picture it would have been hard to tell who was who. In the evening, I would put him on the bed next to Kian and sing to them both. I loved those evenings.

In the fall, I decided to sell the periodontics practice in Lagrangeville. Two periodontists bought it, but a non-compete clause in the sales agreement meant I couldn't practice in Dutchess County for ten years. I took the proceeds and paid off the practice's debt. Then I opened a new office, this one about ninety miles north, and, searching around for pre-owned chairs and pre-owned equipment, I was able to start practicing with no debt at all. But the drive was long, and it felt as if I were once again living out of my car, spending more time on the road than either at home or at work.

With the addition of Kami, it eventually became apparent that our 900 square-foot house in Rhinebeck was going to be too small. We looked around for something bigger and in 2010, we moved to a 3,000 square foot house in the adjacent town of Red Hook. In addition to the extra space, the house was on top of a hill with breathtaking views of the Hudson Valley. The owners of the house were in California and wanted to sell, but winter was coming and they agreed to rent the house to us. They wanted $2,500 a month but I convinced them to take $2,000 by paying a whole year's rent up front, the last of the sales proceeds from the Lagrangeville sale.

By this time, we had found a couple more amazing nurses—Dawn Ginese and Gloria Wood. The pair could not have been more different. Dawn was in her fifties with a grandson on the way. She was bubbly and outgoing. She had a creative side, and played musical instruments and sang professionally. She even had a CD of health songs—a singing nurse. She had been teaching at a Headstart program and was involved in the church her husband Mike had founded. I was so taken by her presence that I immediately hired her. I knew Kian would never be bored with her.

Gloria on the other hand, in her late thirties, was organized and no-nonsense, the type of nurse you want taking care of you if you're seriously sick. In no time she became the lead nurse for us, in charge of the schedule, inventory, bathing Kian, keeping track of doctors' orders, and training new hires. She was my right hand. She was also caring and loving. Both Dawn and Gloria had a love for Kian, and along with Debra, and our other nurses Sharon and Katrina, they tirelessly cared for Kian as their own. They looked out for me, too.

Kian also had amazing teachers, including Diane Cantor from ages one to six, then Sandra Cassada from six onward. Miss Sandy, a speech and language pathologist, was beautiful—petite with blonde hair. Of course, Kian couldn't leave the house very often, so Miss Sandy brought the world to Kian. She spent hours reading to him. Often, she would bring her little poodle Cosmo to the house. Kian loved animals of all kinds, and he especially liked Cosmo. Miss Sandy also took lots of pictures and made albums every year. With her help, Kian graduated from first grade in June of 2013, which, given the circumstances, filled me with as much pride and joy as if he were graduating from Harvard.

Kian also had two wonderful therapists: Terry Rowcroft, his physical therapist, and Lorraine Ricci, his occupational therapist. They worked as a team and made sure that Kian received consistent service and care. And then there was Mark Goldhirsh, Kian's chiropractor. He lived down the road from us and came to the house five mornings a week before going to his office.

All these people were godsends. Their help was invaluable, and I was starting to breathe a bit. It also freed me up to be a mom to Kian, not just a caretaker as I sometimes felt. I pampered him. Gloria bathed him every day, but I came home each night and gave him a shower. Gloria would help me put him onto our shower bed and I would roll him into the shower, calling it our "spa time." I'd have music blasting most of the time—Jackie Evancho or Charlotte Church, or sometimes music from the seventies and eighties. Kian was a good sport and went along with whatever I'd play. I'd wash his beautiful black hair and use a bar of Irish Spring to clean him up. While I'd be doing this, Gloria would change his bed. I bought him the smoothest sheets. And he wore the lightest and purest fabrics. I took care of Kian like a flower.

I still didn't like seeing him spend so much time confined to his bed, so sometimes, I'd prop him up on the couch with pillows at his back, neck, and sides. I got a stander for Kian, too, a stretcher-like piece of equipment that would allow us to put Kian in an upright position. He had to wear orthotic braces on his knees and ankles when we did this because of the added pressure from his weight, but he enjoyed being upright, and I could see how tall and handsome he was getting to be.

When he lost his ability to smile, it was crushing. Just one more thing that SMA took from us. But he could still coo. And when he was unhappy, he would turn red and cry, and we could see from the monitor that his blood pressure was rising. Kian was always hooked to his monitor, giving us a continual fix on his vitals. The monitor showed us his heart rate and, more importantly, his oxygen level. If saliva was building up, impeding his breathing, it needed to be suctioned immediately. Kian would be suctioned almost every five minutes of his life.

Meanwhile, while I was enjoying my time mothering Kian, the marriage was becoming more and more strained. Patrick started drinking even more frequently. Binges were no longer limited to weekends. One weeknight I came home after a twelve-hour day to discover our night nurse resuscitating Kian.

I turned to Patrick. "What's going on?"

With bloodshot eyes and slurring his words, he said listlessly, "Well, Kian seems to be dying again." And apparently, Kami had been crying a lot that day. "And the other one," Patrick added, waving his hand, "was dying earlier."

I jumped in and helped the nurse revive Kian. Then I packed a suitcase and left, taking Kamran with me. I had to trust the night nurse with Kian; I could not stay in the house with Patrick. I drove, crying, to my office where Kami and I spent the night, Kami sleeping soundly in his car seat. At 5 a.m., the nurse called to tell me that Patrick had gone to work, and I went home.

The days went on, but the marriage seemed broken. Patrick and I rarely spoke. I took joy in my two beautiful boys and threw myself into my work.

Chapter 10

Moving On

I THREW MYSELF INTO my work, but I continued feeling guilty every time I left the house for the office. I knew that sacrifices had to be made, however, and it helped to also know that Kian was in good hands.

My new periodontics practice was succeeding and within a year, I was able to open three more locations. I gave up all the other dentist offices I had been working out of and was now, finally, completely my own boss. It was liberating. And in addition to adding locations, I even added a new specialty—endodontics. I knew there was a shortage of endodontics professionals in Upstate New York and I ran some ads in endodontics magazines for a specialist. Soon enough, I hired a recent graduate and my office was now a full-blown periodontics and endodontics office.

At home, things with Patrick kept getting worse. There were times he would disappear on his days off and the nurses would text me saying that he was out and had not been home, or that he was home but seemed drunk. One day, I decided to take things into my own hands. Something had to be done about Patrick's drinking. I called his older sister Cathy in Syracuse and told her that Patrick had a drinking problem, and that I was worried about his health and safety, and the safety of our children. She listened with what seemed like genuine concern, then drove down the next day to talk to him. The two of them went out to dinner and when they came back, they went out on the deck. I was imagining they were having a heart-to-heart talk, but I heard them laughing and carrying on and I soon realized the two of them were doing more drinking than talking. I went to bed. Patrick and Cathy stayed out drinking on the deck until the early hours of the dawn. Without a word to me, Cathy got up the next morning and drove back to Syracuse.

Patrick confided to me that all his family members were alcoholics, something I had not known, something he and his family had been masterful at covering up. I felt deceived and betrayed.

What made it all worse was that I knew what Patrick was like when he was sober. He was funny and kind. He was handy and loved to build things. He spent time outdoors, fishing, swimming, and kayaking in the lake behind our house. He had continued to study Buddhism, attending seminars and reading books. I was hopeful it would help, not just for the sake of the marriage, but for Patrick's own sake. But nothing seemed to be able to pull him away from the lure of the bottle.

One hot summer day, I came home to find him in his Mercedes, parked on the side of the road with the top down. Kamran was strapped into his car seat in the back. A six pack of beer was in the car, too, and Patrick was clearly drunk. A few months after that, I came home to the same thing. Only this time, Patrick wasn't in the car; he was in the house drunk while Kamran was in the car with the doors unlocked, 200 feet from the main road.

Besides the nurses for Kian, I hired a babysitter for Kamran for the evenings, knowing that Patrick was going to drink himself into oblivion every night. When the babysitter moved to California, I decided to hire a live-in au pair. In fact, because the law limited the hours of an au pair to forty-five per week, I hired two of them. This way, I could leave the house with at least some level of comfort that Kamran would be looked after properly.

But soon, I had bigger concerns. Kamran was two and a half, but was not talking. He avoided eye contact. Sometimes, he'd spend time just opening and closing a door. I mentioned all this to one of my dental assistants one day who told me her niece, who acted similarly, had been diagnosed with autism. I went online that night and felt a chill coming over me as I read about the characteristics of autism—lack of social interaction, poor eye contact, repetitive movements. I recognized them all in Kami. The next day, I took him to our pediatrician who referred me to a developmental specialist. The specialist evaluated Kami and confirmed my fears.

Now I had an SMA child, and an autistic child.

I was heartbroken.

Having a child on the autistic spectrum came with its own challenges. I had to enroll Kami in early intervention, and find a program suited for applied behavioral analysis therapy. ABA therapy is based on the science of behavior and learning, helping people with autism to learn actions that can help them acquire necessary social and life skills. Kami's special education teacher had advised me to get a minimum of twenty-five hours of ABA, but when I asked the school board, they initially resisted. ABA therapy was $100 an hour and few school districts would cover twenty-five hours. Nevertheless, by some miracle, our district approved it.

The downside was that the program was forty miles south of Red Hook and I worked ninety miles north. I had to hire a babysitter who would come to the house on weekdays and drive Kami to ABA. For six hours, she'd sit in the waiting room until Kami completed his session. For two years we would do this, until, finally, we could enroll Kami in the local elementary school. In the meantime, I would take Kami to Dr. Kenneth Bock in Red Hook, renowned for his knowledge of autism and ADHD. For the next three years we would follow Dr. Bock's protocols and diets, including IV vitamins and chelation therapy.

The year of Kami's diagnosis, Patrick got laid off from IBM. He spent his days at the mall, at the movies, on his sailboat, and drunk. By 2011, I was ready for a divorce. But I was torn. I was also ready for another baby. I wanted the boys to have a healthy sibling, someone to watch over them if something should happen to me. I put the divorce on hold, hoping that maybe Patrick could get his life straightened out. I had no interest in finding another man, nor did I imagine, with my situation, that another man would be interested in me. I talked to Patrick about having another baby and he agreed, mostly, I came to realize, out of a belief that it wouldn't happen. By then, I was forty-one and he didn't think I could become pregnant. I wondered myself. But in 2012, the unlikely happened. It was going to be another boy. And the CVS test was negative.

During this time, my brother Kia had been trying to play peacemaker, calling me and cajoling me to reach out to our mother. Finally, I did. In fact, we made a trip to Miami so she could meet Kami. It was good to see her but things were clearly not the same between us and I wondered if they ever would be.

Back home, I gave birth to a baby every bit as beautiful as the first two. We named him Cyrus, after my brother. He still held it against me that I'd had him temporarily committed in Miami, but we were on better terms by then, and, for my part, I could never forget all he had done for me. Naming our baby after him seemed entirely appropriate.

Again, I stayed home for only two weeks before going back to work, but this time my mother came to stay with us to help. I was glad. We didn't have a lot to talk about, but we had the kids to take care of, and that gave us common ground. And even though Mom still could not understand my dedication to Kian, she made a point one day that I could not ignore. She saw how I never went out on weekends. For Saturdays and Sundays, I had no nurses on duty during the days and I didn't fully trust the night nurses. So, I would work all week, then come home for the weekend and never leave the house. From Friday evening through Monday morning, it was as if I were on house arrest. Mother's Day came about when Mom was in town, and Gloria volunteered to come over on Sunday so I could take Mom to brunch, a rare moment out.

"Put on some makeup, for God's sake," Mom said as we were getting ready to leave.

"My lipsticks are all expired," I said. "I haven't had the time to buy any new makeup."

Mom went off on this. "You'd better figure out a way to get out of this prison you've made for yourself before you lose your zest for life, Neda! Look at you! You can't even get out of the house! I am eighty years old and even *I* could not live like you do. Is this your dream, Neda? Is this why you spent all those years in school and took on all those student loans? Is this why you left Miami for more excitement in New York?! Wake up girl. Before it is too late!"

I knew she was right. I wasn't getting any younger. Kian needed me, but I had to find a way to grab some moments for myself. I talked to Dawn and Gloria and from then on, they took turns working one of the weekend days, giving me a few precious hours each week to get out of the house and explore the Hudson Valley. I even found the time to buy some new makeup. When Mom was right, she was right.

Cyrus, meanwhile, was progressing very well. He was talking, walking, and potty-trained by the age of two. Cyrus brought me joy and hope. The marriage, on the other hand, continued dying a slow death. There would be no miracle for Patrick. To his credit, he tried AA a couple of times, but he could never stick with it. And if I wasn't completely certain that divorce was inevitable, he made it so, filing for divorce himself in 2014. The filing came as a surprise to me, but I later learned that Patrick had been interviewing attorneys for weeks, seeing who could secure him the best deal. He wanted part ownership of my practice, the practice I'd built while he'd been busy drinking. He wanted ownership of the house that I had borrowed the down payment for. It seemed the only thing he didn't want was custody of the kids.

The divorce proceedings came at a particularly tough time. I had just enrolled in a two-year fellowship implant dentistry program at Columbia University, the very place I had started my career fifteen years earlier. I was taking the 5:30 a.m. train into New York City, sitting in class from 8 a.m. to 5 p.m., and returning home on the late train, just in time to say goodnight to the boys.

Still, I made time for them as best I could. This was the year we took Kian to the beach. We chose Newport Beach in Rhode Island, planning the trip months in advance. Naturally, it was hard taking Kian places. When he was little, I could put him in the red wagon or a stroller by myself. We'd frequently visit state parks on weekends. Now it was more of a production to travel somewhere. Everything had to be arranged just so. For Newport, we rented an RV, which my brother Cyrus drove. Gloria and Dawn came with us, along with our nurse Beth and an au pair.

We checked into a Hyatt on the water, but the rooms they gave us had no beach view. In fact, they were dark, with windows placed high enough up the wall to where Kian could not see out. I told the staff we'd have been better off staying home where Kian could at least have a view of our backyard, but it was Labor Day weekend and all the other rooms were taken. The next day, the hotel manager, seeing our situation, generously took the time to make some phone calls and was able to get us adjoining rooms at the Hotel Viking downtown. We weren't on the beach, but the rooms were big, and the hotel accommodated our every need.

That afternoon, we drove to the nicest beach we could find. It was the first time Kian had ever seen the ocean. We all cheered him as we pushed his wheelchair into the hard sand toward the water. He cooed, watching and listening to the waves and the gulls.

Back home, I had to deal with the divorce. Patrick had lawyered up, and I knew I needed to as well. I found an attorney named Melissa Rutkoske. She was sharp, a graduate of West Point. I wanted her to get a feel for the dynamics of the household and I invited her to meet me at our home. She drove up from Poughkeepsie one afternoon. I introduced her to my mother, who happened to be visiting at the time, Gloria, who was on duty that afternoon, Kian, Kami, Cyrus, and our au pair. She could see immediately the kind of intense care Kian needed, and what was necessary to care for three young boys, two of whom were special-needs kids. She saw how well-run everything was, but she also could tell what kinds of challenges the household faced on a day-to-day basis.

At one point, Mom turned to her and said, "Please help my daughter."

"I'll do everything I can," Melissa promised.

Around this time, Kian began having breathing problems over and above what had been normal for him. I decided a tracheostomy might be the best long-term solution, an air tube inserted into a surgical hole in his neck. This would be much more efficient than a respirator. He'd still need the ventilator to blow air into the trach tube, but the tube would bypass the mouth and vocal cords and go directly to the airway.

At UMDNJ, Dr. Bach tried to talk me out of it. The tracheostomy could lead to infection at the point of insertion, and he cited the case of Christopher Reeve, the *Superman* movie star who'd been paralyzed in a horse-riding accident. He'd ultimately died from complications of an infection, but I knew there was more to the story. There was strong evidence that he'd had an adverse reaction to the antibiotics he'd been given to fight the infection. In reality, Reeve had died of cardiac arrest.

Dr. Bach also suggested that Kian could lose his voice. A helpful nurse at the hospital took me aside and gave me the phone number of an SMA mom who had had a tracheostomy done for her daughter. I called the mom and she reassured me about the procedure, even putting the phone next to her daughter so that I could hear her coo.

I trusted my gut and the tracheostomy helped Kian immensely. Moreover, without the tubes going into his nose, I could see his face more clearly.

Meanwhile, I was still dealing with the divorce. It was moving slowly. A hearing in front of a judge in New York State Supreme Court in Dutchess County finally took place in 2015. Patrick didn't show up but was represented by his attorney. He'd hired a firm that he'd heard advertised on the radio. They'd sent an associate attorney to court. When the judge asked where Patrick was, the attorney said that Patrick was in the Caribbean training for his boat captain's license. This is the first I'd heard that Patrick was not in the States.

The judge, a woman, was clearly annoyed by Patrick's absence, and when Melissa presented our side of things, giving the judge a clear picture of how our household worked—the care that was required for Kian and Kami, the commute I had undertaken to make ends meet, the lack of family support—the judge was even less sympathetic to Patrick.

At a subsequent hearing in February of 2016, almost two years after the legal proceedings had begun for the divorce settlement, the judge finally ruled. Patrick didn't make that hearing either. This time, the judge turned to his attorney and said, "I don't like your client." Then she turned to me and, shaking her head, said, "How do you do it all?" I knew at that moment that she was going to rule for me, but the ruling was even better than I expected. I was granted 100-percent parental rights. The judge ruled that Patrick was an unfit parent. She gave him no rights to my practice, the house, or any property. In fact, I owed him nothing. Patrick ended up with less than what I had offered him at the start of a two-year process that had cost me valuable money and time.

Time, of course, was the costliest element. It had been hard enough to find time to see the kids. By the end of my long days, I had just enough of it to kiss Kian's forehead and ask the nurse how the day had gone. But now it was time to put it all behind me. In May of 2016, the divorce became official. And I was more than ready to move on.

Chapter 11

Death and Romance

EVEN THOUGH I LEGALLY didn't have to, I let Patrick see the boys once every few weeks for a few hours at a time. I thought it was important that the kids maintain a relationship with their dad, and a few hours every now and then seemed to be enough for Kamran and Cyrus as well as for Patrick. One time, however, Patrick asked if he could have the boys spend the night with him on his sailboat. I didn't trust Patrick to stay sober and the boys didn't know how to swim. I told him no way, but I did make it easy for him to visit the boys at the house, and, on a few occasions, I put them all up at a local hotel for the night.

One day, I received a call from my brother Kia. "I need to give you some bad news," he said. "Neda, our brother is gone. Sia passed away yesterday."

This was impossible. Sia was only sixty-three. And he was athletic. He played tennis regularly and had no health issues at all.

"Kia," I said, "what happened?"

"It looks like a suicide," he said. "They found him in his warehouse. He hung himself."

This was even more impossible. Sia was a successful businessman, running an electronics company. He was grounded. He was happy. Suicide? The idea was completely out of character for Sia. There was no way my brother would have taken his own life. I would find out later that shortly before his death Sia paid his taxes. Who pays their taxes before killing themselves? He was seen working out at the gym the very morning of his death. Who does that?

Immediately, I wondered about his wife. She was a Miami socialite. Designer clothes, designer shoes, designer handbags, designer everything. She came from money and was possessive and materialistic. She'd graduated from the University of Miami, but she never worked a day in her life. She spent her time hobnobbing with the elite of South Florida, once making an appearance in the local *Trillionaire Magazine*, where she was shown hanging out at a charity event and making a donation to a cause that we all suspected she probably knew very little about. Nobody in our family liked her. We all thought she was a fake. Nobody could understand what Sia saw in her, and we all sensed that not long into the marriage, it was not a happy one. The pair couldn't have children. The woman put a lot of financial demands on Sia, and there were rumors he had affairs. It's hard to imagine why they stayed married, outside of maintaining a favorable appearance to the jet set that she belonged to.

I was so dumbfounded by the alleged suicide that I contacted the police detective who had been assigned the case. He was convinced Sia had killed himself, and that was that. He had no time for other, less convenient theories. What about an autopsy? That idea would come too late. Sia's wife had his body cremated within forty-eight hours of his death. We didn't even get a chance to see the body, to say goodbye to my beloved brother.

The prevailing notion was that Sia was facing financial problems. But I had seen him face financial problems before. His business was one of ups and downs, and he was the prototypical entrepreneur, riding the ups and downs calmly and coolly. He'd even come back from bankruptcy once. Financial problems were never an issue for Sia. He was much stronger than that. In fact, it was the challenges of the business that he appreciated more than the money. Money didn't mean that much to him. When I was struggling to make ends meet in my first year of dental school, he overnighted me a check for $5,000, telling me to call him if I needed anything more. We learned that a South American company owed Sia half a million dollars and they were not paying him, which, of course, must have put some stress on his cash flow, but we also learned that he had a $5 million line of credit with Pioneer Electronics, his main supplier. No, Sia killing himself over money issues didn't hold up.

Moreover, there was no note to his siblings. There was a short note to his wife but I knew that even if the impossible had actually happened, Sia would have explained his actions to us. He loved us all too much to have left us without saying why.

His wife's actions and attitude didn't help ease our concerns. Besides the quick cremation, she wouldn't let my brother Cyrus and his sister into her home the night of the suicide. Not long after the death, she called me because she needed some information for the death certificate, but her tone made it clear that she thought the whole thing was a nuisance.

I called the detective a few more times, but it was clear he'd moved on. Postulating a murder instead of a suicide would have required opening an investigation that he clearly had no interest in undertaking. Finally, I called Albert Levin, a top-notch Miami criminal attorney, to do some investigating. I hired a probate attorney, too, to try to slow down the liquidation of Sia's assets, which his wife was rapidly doing.

With some pressure from Albert, the police department released to us a copy of the note Sia had left his wife. I sent it to Curt Baggett, a nationally recognized handwriting expert in Texas. He compared the note to samples of writing we had from letters and postcards and handwritten memos that I was able to collect from business associates. The handwriting didn't match.

Finally, we were able to get the Miami police to re-open their investigation, but months had passed by then. The trail was cold. Sia's widow lawyered up and stonewalled the cops, telling them little to nothing. When they went to her building, she refused to let them come up to her condo unit, meeting with them in the lobby instead. An assistant to Sia, who worked in the warehouse, refused to talk to the police. Confidentially, he told us Sia's wife had demanded he say nothing.

While all this was playing itself out, my mother had been back in Iran. We hadn't told her the news. She was now in her eighties, and we knew that hearing of Sia's death would be extraordinarily hard for her, maybe even dangerous to her health. We feared a heart attack or stroke. A few times, in phone conversations with one of us, Mom would ask about Sia. We always told her he was traveling, taking business trips to Venezuela. But one time she scheduled a trip to San Francisco to visit Kia and his wife Nazzi, and we knew that there could be no hiding Sia's death any longer. Mom had a right to know.

I flew to San Francisco with the boys, telling them not to say anything to Grandma about their uncle's death. I took some valium with me and some nitroglycerin. One afternoon, I took my mother shopping, and then brought her back to Kia and Nazzi's house. She complained about her arthritis and that gave me a reason to give her the valium. "This will help," I said. "It's a new kind of pain killer." Then I waited for it to kick in.

"Mom," I said finally, "we have some news." I sat beside her on the couch and continued. "When you were in Iran, something bad happened to Sia."

Right away, Mom said, "Is he gone?"

I nodded. Mom started hitting her legs with the palms of her hand. She wouldn't stop until she was soon out of breath. I put the nitroglycerine pill under her tongue. Kia called 911. The paramedics checked her blood pressure and gave her oxygen. Mom made it through the night, and the next day, and the days after that. But I could see that she would never be the same.

The boys and I flew home, and I reflected on the plane that for the first time, Mom might have understood my love and passion for Kian, how I could never bear the thought of losing him. "If there's a way to pull the plug," she had said years before, "that's what I would do." Faced now with the loss of a son, would she still have said that?

Back in Miami, the police again closed the case. In their estimation, there was no evidence that could definitely prove that anything other than suicide was the cause of our brother's death.

One day, about a year later, Sia's widow drove her Mercedes onto a ferry that ran between exclusive Fisher Island—a residential island with the country's wealthiest zip code—and Miami, a ten-minute ride. She was with a friend of hers, and they remained in the car, the lead car in its lane. It's believed that she had forgotten to put the Mercedes in park. At some point, the car apparently started rolling. In evident panic, she hit the gas instead of the brake. The Mercedes flew through the netting at the edge of the ferry and went nose first into the Atlantic, sending its occupants to the bottom of the channel.

We'll never know for sure if Sia's widow had anything to do with Sia's death, but when we got the news of her accident, we realized that it no longer mattered. If she was innocent, it was a sad story all around—a suicide and a tragic drowning. If she wasn't, it was a karmic debt that had now been paid in full.

—❧✦❧—

One afternoon, not long after Sia's death, I was in the sterilization area when a new assistant for one of the endodontists introduced himself to me. "Hi. I'm Arkady," he said, with a broad smile. "How is your day going?" He was young and handsome, but I was in no mood for socializing.

"Terrible and getting worse," I said.

"Oh, I'm sorry to hear that," he replied with a genuine tone of sympathy, the smile turning into a look of concern.

"I'm sorry," I said, "I don't mean to be negative. I just lost my brother and I guess I'm having a hard time dealing with it."

"Of course."

I didn't think too much of the exchange, but over the course of the next few weeks, Arkady and I would talk from time to time. He was always warm and friendly. It turned out that he was also divorced. He had two kids from the marriage, and it had ended badly. He saw his children when he could, but it wasn't very often.

One night at home, I got a text from him. *Hi, Beautiful.* I laughed it off, assuming he had texted me by mistake. Then came another text. *How was your day?*

I texted back. *Not sure who you're trying to reach, but this is Neda.*

Immediately came another text: *I know.*

I started getting texts from Arkady every night. One night, I decided to finally make him come to the point. "Look," I said, "if you want to ask me out, just ask me out."

Arkady responded, "Okay. Would you like to go out sometime?"

"Sure."

"Where do you want to go?"

"Surprise me."

Arkady lived near Albany. "I'll come down by train on Sunday and we'll take the train into Manhattan," he suggested. "And I'll surprise you."

When Sunday came, we took the train into Manhattan, but then we kept going, all the way to Coney Island. It was a wonderful idea, and the perfect first date. Arkady told me about himself. His parents had moved to the US from Belarus when he was five, and he'd lived in Albany ever since. We walked by the water and Arkady slipped his hand into mine. I felt something for him that I hadn't felt for anyone for a long time. We took the train back and he kissed me before leaving for Albany.

I lay awake that night, wondering how I could possibly squeeze a relationship into my chaotic life. More importantly, why would any man want to be involved in my chaos? Surely, once Arkady began to understand my situation—my three kids, two with special needs, one requiring round-the-clock care—surely, he'd beg off. I told myself not to take it too seriously. I didn't have the time, and Arkady wouldn't have the patience. It was silly to even think about. No, it was clear that there was no way a relationship could ever work.

Chapter 12
Decisions

ARKADY WOULDN'T GO AWAY. Not after meeting the boys, not after learning about Kamran's autism, and not after seeing firsthand the challenges we faced with Kian. If anything, the more we dated, the more he was drawn toward my family rather than from it. I marveled at his interest in the boys, and his patience with me and the lifestyle I was, of necessity, living. He took it all in stride; he was easy and lighthearted and you could feel a positive energy in the house whenever he was visiting.

After several months, Arkady spoke of moving closer. I had no idea how close he had in mind. I said, "Listen, Arkady, sure, I'll help you find a nearby apartment to make it more convenient for us to see each other, but you have to understand that my situation isn't going to change. You've seen my life. It's pretty complicated, and it's not going to get any simpler."

"An apartment?" he chuckled. "No, that's not what I mean by closer. I want to live with you. I want to be here. With you and the boys."

I was speechless. "Live...with me? Here?"

Arkady smiled. "Neda, I love you."

"But—"

"And I love your kids. Can't you see that? I want to be a part of your life."

Arkady didn't move in right away, but he started spending more and more time with us, staying over, sometimes for weekends, and sometimes for longer. The kids loved him. He was like a kid himself. One day he showed up with fishing poles to take Kamran and Cyrus fishing. He'd go to the mall with them and take them to the food court. Around the house, he often acted like another nurse, taking care of Kian, giving him a bath, dressing him, putting him in bed. He seemed to do it all naturally. One evening, we ran out of a medication and Arkady even drove in the night to Albany to a twenty-four-hour drugstore that had what we needed.

At one point, Kamran turned to me and said, "Mom, does Arkady live here now?"

"Well, Kamran," I replied. "I guess he does. What do you think about that? Is that okay?"

Kamran nodded.

Before long, Arkady was a fixture. In fact, with my work schedule, he spent more time at the house than I did. So much so, that he began making friends with the neighbors, people I'd never even had a chance to meet. It was funny to hear him tell me how a few of them, including a prosecuting attorney, had asked what was going on at my place. "We see cars coming and going at all hours," they said. "Different people keep coming in and out." Arkady explained about the nurses and the teachers and my unpredictable schedule. "Don't worry," he told them, laughing. "Neda's not a drug dealer."

In the meantime, my hard work was paying off and my practice continued to grow. I brought in more doctors and we began to run out of space in the main facility. Plus, I didn't like having to drive to the different offices. I made a decision to bring everybody together in one big building, putting the entire practice under a single roof. I found a suitably large building, but it was a former law practice and needed a lot of renovation to make it work for us. I hired an architect and a builder, and we planned a complete building overhaul. The facility would be gutted; all that would remain in place would be the load-bearing walls. When it was finished, it would be the perfect facility for my practice.

But I had enough going on without having to concern myself with the renovation. I trusted the people I'd hired, and all I wanted to do was walk into my new building and get to work. So, while the renovation was taking place, I decided it would be a good time to get away. I'd been wanting to do something for Arkady anyway. His birthday was coming up and I wanted to find a way to thank the wonderful man who had come into my life and made me and the kids so happy. And I knew he hadn't really been anywhere but New York in his whole life.

"Arkady," I asked one day as were watching *Beauty and the Beast* with the boys, "do you have a passport?"

"Sure, I have one."

"Good. You and I are going to Paris."

It took a lot of arranging to make sure everything was covered while we were gone, but we spent a beautiful and romantic week together in Paris, just the two of us, becoming even closer to each other. Then we took a train to the coast of Italy, where we enjoyed the history and charm and beaches of Sanremo. It was wonderful. And by the time we came home, the new building was ready. Everything was perfect.

And that wasn't the end of our traveling together. Two months later, one of the implant companies I did business with was having their annual meeting in Barcelona and they offered me a pair of tickets. How could I refuse? I took Arkady and we had another great time.

Patrick, meanwhile, found out about Arkady when one of the kids told him about the man who took them fishing. He was okay with it; he didn't have a choice, after all, but I was sure that he was as surprised as me that someone would find my crazy life appealing.

One day Kamran told me that as far as he was concerned, Arkady was his dad. I said, "Well then who is Patrick?"

"He's my stepdad," he said. I didn't bother to dispel the idea. To me, it seemed to be just about right.

At the end of that year, Christmas 2018, I decided I wanted Arkady to meet my mother. In spite of everything, it was important to me that she get to know this man in my life. I didn't feel safe going to Iran, so instead, Arkady and I, with Kamran and Cyrus, traveled to Dubai. Mom met us there, bringing my aunt with her, who had just beaten breast cancer. What I didn't know was that Arkady had brought a ring with him. He managed to pull my mom aside at one point and let her know what he was planning, running the idea past her. She gave him her blessing and then he came to me and proposed.

I was moved, but I couldn't say yes. How could I entertain the idea of marriage? My life was full. More than full. Plus, if there was one thing I knew about life, I knew how badly things could go. How could I know that Arkady would still want me after we were married? A divorce, I had learned, is a lot more complicated than a breakup. I said, "I love you, Arkady, but I can't marry you. Not now. I'll tell you what, if we're still together in five years, I'll marry you then."

That was good enough for Arkady. "Whatever you want, Neda," he said. We celebrated Christmas at the hotel where, despite the fact that Dubai is a Muslim country, they had a big Christmas bash complete with a band playing Christmas music and a five-course dinner. I posted pictures on Facebook, which is how my staff back home came to learn of my engagement: in a couple of the photos, my ring was clearly evident.

But then came some terrible news. Not long after our return from Dubai, I received a disturbing text from Melissa Pecorraro, my friend from my old residency days, part of the "sisterhood" we'd created with fellow student Katie Teevan. "Neda," the text read, "wanted to let you know Katie committed suicide. I did not want you to find out on social media." I sat in disbelief, reading the text over several times, certain that my eyes were deceiving me. How could it be possible? My dear friend and colleague was only forty-three years old. She was married, with three beautiful children and a thriving practice.

Arkady and I attended Katie's funeral a few days later where I saw her children for the first time, crying over the loss of their beloved mom. I was overcome with emotion. I wondered what had been going through my beautiful friend's mind, and I felt guilt for not having visited or been in contact with her. Why had she ended her life? Maybe if I had kept in touch, maybe if she had visited and met Kian. She might have talked to me. Maybe, somehow, I could have helped. But now Katie was gone, and nobody would ever really know why.

As for my life, changes were coming. Arkady and I had a conversation one day and decided we'd like to have a baby, one of our own. But I was forty-nine and it was not an easy decision. One good thing was that I was quite familiar by then with the in vitro fertilization process, not that I was looking forward to going through it again. Because of my age, the doctor advised making use of not one, but three embryos. I balked, wondering what would happen if all three survived to term. Instead, I agreed to two. Of course the idea was that only one of the two would become viable. The chances of both doing so were low.

But that's exactly what happened.

I became pregnant with twins.

The doctor strongly cautioned me not to try to bring both to term. "You've had multiple pregnancies," he said.

"You've had multiple C-sections. Plus, you're forty-nine. You could risk losing both of them."

I decided to wait until the results of the embryo testing came back. If one were genetically defective, my decision would be made for me.

Both results came back healthy.

Then I decided to consider gender. I had nothing but boys. This time, I wanted a girl.

Both were determined to be girls.

I agonized over what to do. The doctor was pushing for aborting one of the fetuses. "Selective reduction" was the euphemism he used. Arkady and I discussed it at length, with him saying he would abide by whatever decision I wanted to make. Finally, I gave in to the doctor.

Almost immediately, I regretted it. So did Arkady. Had we just eliminated the life of a potentially healthy baby? On the other hand, what if the doctor was right? What if keeping them both would have resulted in the loss of both? I found myself feeling resentful that I even had to make such a decision. Nobody should have to make a life and death choice like that. Nevertheless, the decision had been made and we had to move on.

Around this time, Dawn, one of my top nurses and a woman who had become a dear friend, announced to me that she was considering retirement. I could do nothing but wish her well, keeping to myself what a loss her retirement would mean. Fortunately, a couple of months later, she said she'd had a slight change of heart and wanted to continue on a part-time basis. I was thrilled and relieved. But it made me realize how dependent I had become on my nurses. Dawn and Gloria and Debra were indispensable, but I began thinking I should be closer to Kian at all times just in case something happened. Plus, I had a baby on the way. I no longer wanted to work too far from home.

As it happened, the building I had renovated was on a large plot of land, large enough to build a house next to the facility. Soon, I had engineers planning the house and obtaining the required permits. It was going to be the perfect set-up. I would never have to drive to work again; I would be able to walk to my office every morning.

Ideally, the house would have been built before the baby arrived, but I knew the construction would take too long. I couldn't wait. I rented a house close to the office and moved us all there, pending the completion of our new home. My mother came to visit and helped us pack. One Sunday morning, with Gloria on hand, Mom and I were packing everything into boxes, and I noticed Gloria, sitting in a chair, begin to nod off.

"She must be really tired," I commented to Mom. "I've never known her to fall asleep on the job."

And then I watched as Gloria slid off the chair onto the floor. I ran over and held her head up as she vomited. "I think I'm having a stroke," she managed to say in a halting voice.

"Arkady!" I yelled out, "Call 911!"

The paramedics came and put Gloria into the ambulance and took her to Northern Dutchess Hospital, from which she was soon sent to the trauma center at Vassar Brothers Medical Center. We followed, and I cried and prayed the whole way. Gloria was only forty-six. I realized with a shudder that if it would have been a weekday, she would have been at the house alone. Arkady and I both would have been at work, and Gloria would probably have died in our home.

I visited her and her husband Carlos in the intensive care unit as much as I could. Eventually, Gloria was cleared to be transferred to a rehab center, but I knew it was going to be a long road to recovery for her.

In the days and weeks that followed, I found myself distraught by Gloria's stroke and anxious about the future. Being pregnant didn't help. I was on an emotional roller coaster and cried at seemingly everything. At one point, needing some sort of assurance that the future was going to be okay, I contacted Stacey Wolfe again, the New York City psychic who had told me to pull myself together, stop feeling sorry for myself, and enjoy being a mom to Kian. The one who had predicted—correctly—that Kian would live into his teens.

"Gloria is going to be fine," she said. "It might take a while, but she's going to be okay."

I breathed a sigh of relief and stifled the tears I felt coming on.

But then Stacey continued, "But, Neda," she said, "by the time she comes back, I don't think you'll need her."

"What do you mean?" I said. "Gloria has been so important to us. Why wouldn't I need her?"

"Because of Kian," she said.

"Because of Kian?"

"Yes. I'm sorry, Neda. This might be hard to hear, but I don't see Kian being here by the time Gloria comes back." And then, before I could say anything, or even get my thoughts together, she concluded, "I'm afraid Kian will be gone, Neda. Your boy will be gone."

Our call ended. I hung up the phone and felt the tears coming on again. This time, I couldn't stop them. I didn't even bother to try.

Chapter 13
A Hundred Times

GLORIA WAS AN INDEPENDENT nurse; she had no unemployment, nor did she have disability. In no time, she was in financial trouble. For three months, while she was rehabbing, I continued to pay her salary, and I was happy to. Gloria had done so much for our family. She had never missed a day. She took one vacation in the whole time she had worked for us, and that vacation had almost been ruined. She and two friends had booked a cruise, but their flight to get to the port had been canceled at the last minute and they couldn't catch another one. The ship left without them. Gloria called from the airport and told me she would be working after all; her vacation—her one vacation—had been scrubbed. I could hear the dejection in her voice. "Sit tight," I told her. "You're going on vacation." Then I called my travel agent and booked a flight for her and her two friends to Mexico for an all-expenses-paid vacation. If anyone deserved it, it was Gloria.

Now she was really struggling. The three months of salary I continued to pay helped, but sometime after that, I got word that she wasn't able to make ends meet. She'd asked a mutual friend for $300 to help her pay her rent. When I heard that, I overnighted her a check for $5,000. Gloria had not only been an amazing nurse and close friend, she'd become a part of the family. How could I not help a family member in distress? Besides, I thought of the time Sia had sent me $5,000. Now I was paying his gift forward.

In the meantime, I kept working, trying hard not to think about Stacey Wolfe's heartbreaking words to me about Kian. Maybe she was wrong this time, I thought. She can't be right all the time.

Soon, we moved into the house I'd rented. It was an old house, but it had a handicapped-accessible bathroom, which was critical, one of the main reasons, besides location, that I had chosen it. To properly bathe Kian, we needed to roll him into the shower on a special shower gurney. But not long after moving, I began to develop a hacking cough. There were times when I couldn't stop coughing, and I was sure I'd somehow developed asthma. My doctor couldn't find anything wrong with me, but the coughing persisted.

One day, Cyrus and Kamran set up a lemonade stand in front of the house. I happened to be outside when a neighbor dropped by. I introduced myself and she said, "How's the mold in your house? We recently had to hire a mold removal service."

"Mold?"

"Yep, these are all old houses," she explained. "There are so many trees around, and it stays pretty damp around here. Mold is a real problem."

I called the landlord who assured me that our house had no mold, but I suddenly had a likely explanation for my coughing fits. I called a mold inspection company who confirmed my suspicions. Fixing the problem would have taken too long, even if I could have gotten the landlord to do it. My baby was due in two weeks. I rented an apartment and once again we moved. The apartment was small and certainly not ideal, but it would have to do. It was on the ground floor, and the shower, though not built to be accessible, was big enough to roll Kian's shower bed into. There were two bedrooms, a small living area, and a dining room, which became a supply room for all of Kian's stuff. All the rest of our belongings went into storage.

Early one morning, very close to my due date, I woke up in pain. Arkady drove me to the hospital, where they told us everything was fine and sent us home. The same thing happened the next day. This time, they did an ultrasound and determined there was not enough fluid for the baby. The baby needed to come out right then. They rushed me into a delivery room and did a C-section. Moments later, I was holding our daughter. Leila was a healthy, seven-and-a-half-pound baby. And beautiful—like a rose wrapped in a pink blanket, as I would tell my mother. Arkady and I were joyful, but in the back of my mind, I couldn't help but think of the choice we'd made earlier and wonder if perhaps we should have been welcoming twins into the world that day.

After I recovered, I went back to work. But Leila came with me. I took one room we weren't using and made a nursery out of it, hiring a babysitter to watch Leila when I was seeing patients. I loved spending the precious time between patients with my daughter.

For Kian, I hired new nurses to accommodate the loss of Gloria who was still recovering. When she did come back, I hired her daughter-in-law, a nurse's aide, to accompany her, to be her arms and legs until she fully recovered. It took some effort to lift and move Kian around. And I kept the new nurses to cover the night shift. Everything was now running smoothly. Gloria was back, Kian was being taken care of, and we had our new baby. I stopped thinking about Stacey Wolfe's prediction. Life was good.

Leila was born on August 27, 2019. Construction started on our new house in February of 2020. We designed it with Kian in mind. It was spacious, with wide doors, and outlets everywhere for all his equipment. We could easily move him anywhere. The time had come to sell our house in Red Hook. This was bittersweet. After all, the kids had spent most of their childhoods in that house, and we had some wonderful memories, but all of us were excited about our new home.

Something else was going on in February of 2020. What had started out as a few worrisome cases of a virus in China a few months earlier had spread around the globe. Thousands had died and many more thousands had been hospitalized. At the time, there was no vaccine and no real consensus on how to stop the virus's spread. Everything seemed to be shutting down because of COVID. Sports leagues, schools, businesses—cities became like ghost towns.

I kept my practice open. I ordered personal protective equipment for everybody, and I stopped bringing Leila in. At home, I made sure all the nurses were masked and outfitted with PPE. It was not an easy time, but it was important to me that things run as close to business-as-usual as possible.

The weeks and months rolled along. The new house was taking shape. One night in June, I looked in on Kian before going to bed. The night nurse was coming on duty and all was well. It had been another long day and I dropped into bed and fell into a restful sleep.

At four o'clock in the morning, the nurse knocked on our bedroom door and woke me up. "Everything is okay with Kian," she said, "but I think something is wrong with the ventilator."

The ventilator had an alarm, which I had been conditioned to hear. No matter how deep a sleep I was ever in, the alarm would jolt me from my bed and send me rushing to Kian. But I had heard no alarm that night.

I darted into the living room where Kian was. Everything was *not* okay with him. He was blue, almost gray. His oxygen level was below 25 percent. I ran to get the backup ventilator but putting him on it made no difference. I used the oxygen tank, but he still didn't respond.

"Arkady!" I screamed. "Get the paramedics here!"

Arkady called 911 and the paramedics came in no time. They loaded Kian, unconscious, into the ambulance, and I rode with him to the hospital.

There, the ER staff jumped into action, doing everything they could. I thought about all the close calls of the past, all the episodes, all the times Kian had needed to be resuscitated. All the times we'd cheated death. I thought about Stacey Wolfe's prediction and I had a terrible sense, even before anyone in the ER could tell me, that our chances had run out. We would cheat death no more.

As I watched, Kian slipped away. Finally, the doctor in charge approached me, telling me what I already knew.

"I'm sorry," he said.

I went over to Kian and held him, my tears streaming down as his frail body became colder.

Kian had been born perfect—a beautiful, healthy baby boy. Eight weeks afterward, he had been diagnosed with spinal muscular atrophy. But he had never stopped being perfect to me. The doctor at the time said he wouldn't live past his second birthday. I did everything I could do to prove him wrong and to give my Kian the highest quality of life possible, knowing he deserved no less. But at that moment, knowing I'd done my best—and knowing that Kian had outlived the doctor's prediction by a dozen years—gave me little comfort. In the back of my mind, I'd always known this day would someday come, but of course, how could one have ever prepared for it? I cried uncontrollably. The staff was good enough to leave us alone and I sat with Kian for some time, unwilling to part with him.

Finally, I rose, knowing I needed to call Patrick, my family members, and the other nurses. I had to break to them the news I could not yet grasp myself: Kian, my beautiful boy, was gone.

Later, I would take note of the date. It was my father's birthday. I'd always thought there was so much of Kian that reminded me of my dad: same complexion, same eyes, same hair. The date somehow seemed more than coincidence.

Arkady's niece drove to the apartment to watch the kids and Arkady came to join me at the hospital. I called Patrick and told him the news and he soon came. He cried, and I thought about when we were together and I'd been pregnant with Kian. We had been so happy. So young. We had been so excited about life's possibilities. That all seemed like a million years ago. Patrick kissed Kian's face and left.

I called my siblings. Mom was in Miami visiting and I talked to her, too. Then I called Gloria and Debra and Dawn. Then Arkady drove us home as the sun rose on a new day—a day without Kian. A different world now.

The boys were up by the time we entered the apartment and they asked how their brother was doing. I hadn't thought about what to say. I wasn't ready to say anything. "He's not doing very well," I told them, trying to keep it together. "But he's in the hospital and they're keeping an eye on him." I'd break the news to them at some point, but I knew I had to get my thoughts together first.

Later that morning, I called a funeral home. Only twice had I had any experience with a funeral—once when I'd sat in my car in the parking lot of the funeral home in Miami when my uncle had died, unable to bring myself to go inside, and once when I attended my friend Katie's funeral. Now I had to make funeral arrangements for my son.

Afterward, I phoned Kian's doctor and told him what had happened. He suggested an autopsy. Setting aside the SMA, Kian had been healthy. He had been fine that day, and fine when I saw him before going to bed that night. There was no reason for what happened to have happened. What could have gone wrong?

I also wondered about the ventilator alarm. Why hadn't I heard it? I was furious at myself when I thought I might have slept through it. But the ventilator had the equivalent of a black box that stored forty-eight hours of data, and I sent it off to the company for a report.

Together, the autopsy and the ventilator report would provide a heartbreaking account of Kian's death. As it happened, the alarm had gone off, just as it was supposed to. Twenty-eight times. Each time, the nurse turned it off. She had tried to resuscitate Kian but had neglected to turn off his feeding tube. As she resuscitated him, formula was drawn into his lungs. Kian had drowned. The nurse didn't call 911, and by the time she came to get me, it was too late.

I finally told the boys. Cyrus probably had assumed the worst. From his bedroom, he'd heard me crying while we'd been waiting for the ambulance that night. "And I cried, too, Mommy," he told me. They wanted to know where Kian was going to be buried, but I had other plans. I couldn't live with the thought of leaving him in the ground somewhere. Kian needed to be with me. I decided to have him cremated, and when I die, Kian will be buried with me. It was the same decision Deborah Heine had made for her daughter Claire.

I went to the funeral home before the cremation, and they kindly let me spend a few minutes alone with Kian. I kissed his head and said, "Thank you for being my kid. I'm so sorry I couldn't save you." I thought about the day he'd been diagnosed with SMA, how crushing it was. All his life, I had tried to undo his condition. I had wished he was as healthy as anybody else's kid. And standing there beside his body that day, I found myself feeling ungrateful. "I'm sorry," I told him through my tears. I knew at that moment that I would have gladly gone through it all over again, exactly as it had all happened. "A hundred times," I said to him. "I'd take you back, just as you were, a hundred times."

And then I backed out of the room, slowly, looking at Kian the whole time, unwilling and unable to take my eyes off him. I hesitated at the door, thinking that I wanted to stay with him forever, to go with him, to have my body cremated with his. And then I thought back to Katie's funeral, the vision of her children crying at the loss of their mother. I couldn't leave my children. I knew that at least with Katie, she had a strong, extended family to provide support for her kids, something I didn't have. They needed me, and I knew it. I knew I had to focus not on the loss, but on the life of Kian and the time I had gotten to spend with him. I finally left the room, wiped away my tears, and drove back to the apartment, deciding that I would be grateful now. Grateful for all of it.

Chapter 14

My Angel

FOR TWO WEEKS, I'D wake up every morning at 4 a.m., the time when the nurse had awakened me the day Kian had died. Sometimes I'd be able to go back to sleep. Other times, I'd get up and go into the living room where Kian's bed still rested, along with all his equipment. I would sit there and listen to the stillness. A few times I lay on his bed, smelling his sheets and weeping silently so as not to wake anyone up. Everything in the room was exactly the way he'd left it. All that was missing was Kian.

It was the middle of COVID and my siblings used that as an excuse not to come see us. I was hurt. I got more support from my wonderful nurses. Dawn made sure I had a copy of all the photos she'd taken of Kian, even making a collage of photos for the boys, and sending them cards. Dawn and Gloria and Debra were more family to me than my own siblings.

I received support from others, too. Donna Schulte, the Red Hook school psychologist who had been instrumental in coordinating an individualized educational program for Kian, came to the apartment a few days after getting the news. She had a card that had been signed by all the teachers and therapists who'd come to the house over the years to work with Kian. I had always referred to Kian as my "Persian Prince." "Kian," in fact, is Persian for prince. The card read, "Now your Prince is with the King."

Donna turned to me and said, "I want to say something to you, Neda. Years ago, when I first met you, you said to me you were going to do everything you could do for Kian. You did just that. You did the best you could. I hope you can move on without any feelings of guilt. You did an amazing job with your son, Neda. Don't you dare feel any regret."

It was a profoundly touching thing to say at a moment when I needed to hear it.

And then came something more profound. Back when I had decided to carry two embryos, allowing one to come to term—Leila—there had been that third embryo. We had kept it frozen. After having made the heart-wrenching decision to abort the one embryo, I decided not long after Leila's birth that I wanted that third embryo implanted. Deep down, I knew the chances of viability were slim—most likely the embryo would not even survive to be transferred—but at least I wouldn't have to feel any guilt about discarding it.

The very morning of Kian's passing, I received a phone call from the fertility clinic. "It's viable," they told me. "We have you scheduled for the transfer on Monday."

It was obviously a lot to take in. My son had just died; now I was scheduled for implantation, to become pregnant again. It was extraordinarily difficult, but I kept the Monday appointment, crying at times, and telling the staff I was just being overly emotional. I knew if I told them the truth—that I was mourning the loss of my son—they would send me home. On this day, I acted like some of my dental-phobic patients when I'd tell them they were about to have a tooth extracted. I figured the nurses would just shake their heads at the hormonal woman before them.

The next day, distraught, confused, and in need of some sort of direction, I reached out to a medium in Poughkeepsie that I had heard on the radio. Deborah Hanlon's readings were in extreme demand. I sent an email, but mostly expected that I wouldn't hear back. To my surprise, an assistant of hers replied telling me that Deborah would be available the following afternoon by phone—Wednesday, two days after the transplantation and just a few days after Kian's passing.

I knew I couldn't place the call in my office. It would be too emotional and I didn't want anyone overhearing. I left the office at the appointed time and called Deborah from my car in the parking lot. Deborah dove right in. "Your son wants you to know that you should not be thinking that you should have gone with him." I *had* thought that. I'd felt it when I was holding his body. *Why can't I go too?* "Your son wants you to know he's in a great place," continued Deborah. "He can walk now. He can run." Tears were welling in my eyes. "And he knows you're going to have another baby." My mouth flew open. There was no way Deborah could have known that. "Your son says it's your consolation prize." Then she finished with this: "Kian loves you very much and thanks you for all that you did for him."

I hung up and sat in my car crying, but for the first time, these were not tears of mourning. I felt elated; I felt blessed.

A week later, the fertility clinic confirmed the pregnancy. The implantation had been successful and the due date would be the following February, right around my birthday.

But at the office, things became very stressful one day. My manager motioned me into her office and announced she was leaving. "I don't think this is the career for me," she said. "It's just not working out like I'd thought it would." Then she talked about opening a yoga studio. I was floored. I'd had no idea. She agreed to stay on for thirty days, but this was in the middle of a pandemic. I knew how difficult it was going to be to replace her, and her role in the practice was critical.

I left her office and went into mine and my mind started racing. It was too much to take, especially on the heels of all that had recently transpired. Then I noticed I was bleeding. A little at first, and then more. I called my doctor who told me to go to the E.R. There, they did ultrasounds and informed me that I was in the middle of a miscarriage.

It was devastating news and I wondered how much devastation one person could take.

"Can the baby not be saved?" I asked.

The doctor on duty frowned and said, "I'm sorry, but it's very unlikely."

I was admitted for the night, and a D and C—a dilation and curettage procedure—was scheduled for the next morning to clear the uterus. I called Arkady who had his brother watch the kids while he visited with me in the hospital. We both cried.

The floor I was on was the maternity floor, making the whole situation more painful. Mothers were having healthy babies in rooms filled with stuffed animals and balloons, walls decorated with happy characters and images.

It was a place of joy, and I was there for all the wrong reasons.

An understanding nurse came in the middle of the night and talked to me. "Do you have faith?" she asked at one point.

"Well, kind of," I said. "But I've been through so much."

She nodded and then said a prayer while I wept for the baby I would not have.

By the morning, the bleeding had stopped and they did an ultrasound in preparation for the D&C. But they didn't do the D&C. The ultrasound was a revelation.

"The baby has a heartbeat," the doctor smiled at me. "You're going to be fine."

Deborah Hanlon had been right. The doctors—science—had been wrong.

I called my mother on the way home and filled her in on what had happened. "It was God," I told her. And I believed it. I had never felt the presence of God before, but I felt it that morning. I changed clothes and went to work, not caring any longer about the manager leaving or any of the other problems that now seemed so small and unimportant.

Our healthy son was born a week after my birthday. We named him Sia after my late brother. Sia Kian. My consolation prize. My gift. My confirmation that an angel is looking over me. A beautiful angel, who can walk and run now, and who, I happen to know, remains as grateful as I am for the time we spent together here on earth.

Epilogue

WE NEVER HAD A funeral for Kian. Instead, on September 18, on what would have been his fourteenth birthday, with the help of Dawn, we held a celebration of life at a nearby park. I brought a photo that Dawn had once taken of Kian all dressed up. I had the photo enlarged and framed with "Persian Prince" written at the bottom, and we sat it on a park table and gathered around it. We had catered food and balloons, and exchanged memories of Kian. I invited Dawn's husband Mike, who was a pastor and who said a few words. Then Dawn and others took turns talking about my prince. Patrick even came by, but he stood like a stranger at a distance, not saying much or sharing anything about Kian.

The day was special and before it ended, I decided that we'd celebrate Kian's birthday every year.

By then, our house was ready for us to move into, the house right next to my practice. The house we'd built with Kian in mind—spacious, with wide doors, and outlets everywhere for all his equipment. We set up his bedroom and we all called it Kian's room, even though he would never live there. Even still, we sensed his presence.

I still owned my nursing agency and, in fact, by then it had become officially licensed by the state of New York for skilled nursing and nutrition. Ironically, I received the official license in the mail about a month after Kian passed away. With COVID, I needed to bring the agency up to date with the new standards or risk losing the business. I decided to stick with it and took on more cases of kids with rare conditions, extending the company's reach from one county to seven. To think that the agency was started by a little boy with SMA. Ultimately, I transferred the ownership to one of Kian's nurses and her husband.

One day in October of 2022, I realized I hadn't heard from Patrick for a while. He'd missed Kami's birthday, but it wasn't completely unusual for that to happen. Still, it seemed strange that so much time had gone by without any communication. I texted him, but the text came back as undeliverable. Then I went on Facebook and saw pictures he'd posted in September of him and a new girlfriend somewhere in the Caribbean where he'd been sailing and hiking. They looked happy, the cruise explained his whereabouts, and I thought no more about it. Then, toward the end of October, a letter in a priority mail envelope arrived.

It was from Patrick's son Eric, and I felt my heart sink as I read the words: "I have sad news to pass along to you and the boys. Dad passed away a few weeks ago." I was stunned. Arkady came home from being out with the kids and I pulled him aside and told him to take the kids back out somewhere. I didn't want them to see me as I was at that moment.

Later, I would talk to Eric and find out that Patrick had died of a cardiovascular event—either a stroke or a heart attack. It had happened at sea and there had been no way to get him help. It seemed so unfair to me. Had it happened on land, maybe he'd have had a chance. Maybe it would have served as a warning for him, to change his lifestyle, to stop drinking, or to at least take some sort of action that, now, he would have no chance to take. When we were married, I used to kid him about not taking better care of himself. "I hope you have life insurance," I would say.

"Why?" he'd reply, "are you planning on having me whacked?"

"Oh, no, I want you to live a long life and suffer!"

Now Patrick was gone. We'd had our differences, but at one time, he had been my husband. At one time, we had been in love. And for good or for bad, he was the father of my children. I remembered back to our first date, the walk we took in Weehawken along the river. He'd asked if he could hold my hand.

Patrick was sixty-three years old. Later, I would learn of the date of his death: September 18. Kian's birthday.

The weeks went by, and I came to realize that the only thing that had kept me in New York was Kian. His nurses, the doctors, the therapists, his teachers. Even Patrick. There was really nothing keeping me there any longer and maybe it was time to move on. I started thinking about other places we could live. And then I remembered visiting Charleston, South Carolina for my certification class years before. I had fallen in love with the city, with the charm of its historic buildings and its cobblestone streets. I had strolled those streets with Kian and made a promise to myself that I would one day return. Now, that day had come.

I sold my practice and we all moved to just outside of Charleston. We live there happily today, the move representing a new beginning for all of us. And, by the way: one of Stacey Wolfe's predictions? I would one day live somewhere where the sun shines most of the year. Looks like she was right once again.

I'd never forgotten my promise to Arkady. I told him when he proposed to me in 2018 that we would marry in five years if we were still together. It's a promise I'm going to keep. As I put the finishing touches on this book, we are planning our wedding. He's been such an integral part of my life that family and friends may be surprised by the wedding, believing us already married. And why not? I've been referring to Arkady as my husband for quite some time now. Soon, it will be official. More wonderful news: Kami, autism and all, is set to attend the Charleston Charter School for Math and Science. Back in 2010, when he was diagnosed, this would not have seemed possible. His plan is to pursue a career in engineering, and I have no doubt he will be successful.

Mom lived in Jacksonville, Florida for a couple of years with Cyrus, and Pari, who moved to the States permanently. Jacksonville was a three-and-a-half-hour drive away, but we saw very little of my mother. There always seemed to be some reason or another why she could not come to see me and her grandchildren. She came to New York before we moved, but it was after our celebration of life for Kian, which she missed. And the primary reason for her visit was because Arkady had found her a doctor to perform back surgery that she needed. Ironically, she stayed in Kian's room to recuperate. I mentioned this to Gloria who said, "Kian brought your mom back and had her stay in his bed."

Regardless of her reason for coming, I was happy to see Mom, even if our relationship had changed. By then, she had stopped offering me her advice on family matters, not so much out of respect for my own ability to make judgements about my life and family, but because I think she basically gave up.

Since then, with Cyrus and Pari, she has moved back to Miami where our lives in the US started some forty years ago. I helped them renovate the house I had bought years ago and we put in a pool. I take the kids and we visit when we can. My relationship with Mom is civil, but cool. She has never understood my relationship with Kian and my desire for him to live, and I know she never will. On the other hand, I am in this country and living my life because of my mother and what she did for me. What she did for our whole family.

I wonder sometimes what would have become of me had we remained in Iran, a country where women have almost no rights. Educational opportunities are limited. The legal age of marriage for a girl is nine and many young women are still forced into arranged, loveless marriages where the husbands have complete power, wives are considered property, and violence against a wife is legal. Nothing has changed since my mother was married away seventy-five years ago. If anything, things are worse. For women, hijabs are required in public, and refusal to wear one can mean a ten-year prison sentence. Recent protests and demonstrations have revealed the strength and courage of Iranian women, but at the cost of torture and the killing of many of those who have dared speak up.

Mom knew I would have no life in Iran if we stayed. She got me out. She got my brothers out. "You have to get an education," she told me repeatedly, wanting for me a better life than she had. Her life was challenging and she made many sacrifices for us. Maybe she's not an SMA mom, but she's a mom, and the love for her children was always the lodestar for her, guiding her decisions. And besides all of that, there was her undeniable strength, a trait she passed along to me. Without it, I could not have faced half of what I faced.

I picked up strength from my grandmother, too, a woman whose husband Mohamad Amin Azadivatan had been executed by government guards, taken from her in the middle of the night. He was hanged and his lifeless body had been dragged through the snow in the streets of Iranian Azerbaijan. He was a true freedom fighter, a servant of the underdog, and whose legacy led to multiple published books. Because of him the entire Azadivatan family was banned from any governmental jobs for decades to come. In his last speech, right before he was killed, he said, "I am a pine tree; I bend but I do not break." Grandma Monie had more than strength. She had faith. "Someday, Neda," she would tell me, "you will realize everything on your own. God has a plan for you."

I ceased to believe in God not long after Kian was diagnosed with SMA. None of my prayers were answered, so I stopped praying. Feeling like a hypocrite, I would take the other kids to church for Easter egg hunts and Christmas mass, going through the motions, almost laughing at what I perceived to be the sham of religion.

Looking back over my life now, it's impossible to not see that God was with me the whole way. Stacey Wolfe and Deborah Hanlon have shown me that there is much more to this universe than meets the eye, and I marvel at the moments when God was clearly present, starting when Jafar took me in as his own daughter. Because of his generosity, I had a family. And God was present when I was able to live in Italy and learn a second culture and language. And the time I was able to leave Iran—safely in the midst of a war—to travel to the United States for the opportunities most girls in Iran can only dream about. And when I was accepted to the University of Miami and had loving brothers who supported me so I could attend full time and then move on to dental school. Yes, there was a lot of debt, but that, too, seemed a part of the plan, ultimately forcing me to be more resourceful and enterprising. And, yes, I had my heart broken when the man I loved told me he didn't love me back, but that made way for another love, and, in time, the love of my life.

God, I can now see, was even present at the Westchester Medical Center in the very first week after Kian's diagnosis. The priest came to see me there, to advise that I baptize Kian. I resisted initially. "If there is a God, why is this happening to an innocent baby?" I asked. God has a plan, he told me, reminding me of Grandma Monie's words. I had Kian baptized, but then came all the doubts about God. What I couldn't see at the time was the strength God had given me to survive those early days.

Later, I would see God in other moments. It was God who sent me all those angels—Dawn, Gloria, Debra, Miss Sandy, not to mention other angels like Katrina Cole, Yoshada Shiwdin, Melissa Thompson, and Janine Ardohain. It was God who helped save Kami's life during the emergency C-section. It was God who placed Sharon in the pediatric intensive care unit at Westchester Medical to take care of Kami during our stay there. It was God who put DeAnna Reasor Weekes in my path to become my right hand in setting up my own nursing and billing companies. It was God who helped me establish a successful practice in upstate New York where people from as far away as 200 miles would come see me. It was God who helped me find and purchase the best house in Red Hook to meet Kian's needs. It was God who helped me pay for all those vacations for Kian and his nurses. It was God who helped me get the best outcome in the divorce. It was God who helped me get the best care for Kamran's autism. It was God who, after four years of infertility treatments, allowed me to have Cyrus. It was God who helped me save Leila from a selective reduction procedure. It was God who helped me deliver a healthy baby boy at the age of fifty-one.

It was God who held me at the funeral home. And held me up. Kian and I were not alone there. It was God again when I ended up in the hospital for a near miscarriage, saving the baby. It was God who saved me from a pulmonary embolism while I was pregnant.

God was revealed to me so many times, and yet, amazingly, it wasn't until Sia that I became convinced. Today I have faith. My son Cyrus has become a Christian. I was raised a Muslim and Arkady is Jewish, but we go to church with Cyrus every Sunday. The religion doesn't matter so much to me. What matters is the belief. None of these things and people that came my way were coincidences. I no longer believe in coincidences.

Many of us don't believe that there is a God and we are either too cynical or too proud to put our faith in God's plan. Even if we go to church, we don't properly engage in God's glory. We frequently drift away, especially when things do not go our way. But what I had initially believed was a curse from a cold, loveless universe was, in actuality, a blessing from a loving God. Kian gave me purpose and drive. He gave my life meaning. He taught me to never give up. Though he couldn't walk, couldn't talk, couldn't even sit up, he was my powerhouse of strength. And he opened my heart to motherhood. On our last Mother's Day, the nurses arranged his gift for me: a framed picture of Kian with the words, "You inspire me." But in reality, it was the other way around. Kian inspired me, and still does.

And yet, for all his strength, he was a gentle soul. He made me a mom for the first time and taught me to love unconditionally. He taught me to never take anything for granted. I learned never to complain or stress about the little things. I learned to be happy that I can walk, eat, and breathe without machines.

Kian taught me gratitude.

When I think of Kian, I don't see a helpless child confined to a bed. I see the greatest teacher I could ever have been blessed with.

Resources and Ways to Help

In May of 2022, the FDA approved a treatment for SMA through gene replacement therapy. The therapy, with the brand name of **Zolgensma**, is not a complete cure and cannot reverse damage that SMA has already done to a patient's motor neurons, but Zolgensma *can* stop the progress of the disease. And if SMA is caught early enough, Zolgensma can be as good as a cure for an infant who would otherwise have to suffer the ravaging muscular effects of this devastating condition. Unfortunately, though it's a one-time intravenous treatment, Zolgensma currently comes with a price tag of over $2 million. Not every insurer covers it.

Additionally, there is **Evrysdi**, an oral prescription medication that replaces the missing protein in children or adults with SMA, improving muscle strength. It is not a cure, but it does allow some relief from the debilitating symptoms. A drug that works similarly is **Spinraza**. Spinraza is administered as an intrathecal injection where the medication is injected into the cerebrospinal fluid of the spine.

If you'd like to know how you can help those in need of this therapy, or would like further information about Spinal Muscular Atrophy, its testing, treatment options, or what helpful resources might be available, please visit these sites:

Cure SMA provides support to patients and families affected by spinal muscular atrophy, and funds and directs research: https://www.curesma.org

Jadon's Hope Foundation, a nonprofit organization that promotes educational awareness and funds research efforts: http://www.jadonshope.org/

Miracle for Madison Fund, under the Ohio State University Foundation, is a grassroots, volunteer group raising money to support research and clinic services for SMA at OSU: http://www.miracleformadison.org/

SMA News Today, and its parent company Bionews, provide the SMA community with vital news & important information: https://smanewstoday.com

One SMA voice, a spinal muscular atrophy community with resources and a "Social Wall" message board: https://www.onesmavoice.com/

SMA My Way, a collaboration to support people impacted by SMA with practical tools and empowering connections: https://www.smamyway.com

SMA Foundation, established in 2003 by SMA parents with a mission to accelerate the development of treatments: https://smafoundation.org/about-us/

SMA Angels Charity, an organization that supports crucial SMA research, offers support to SMA families, and advocates and for SMA: https://www.smaangels.org/

Made in the USA
Columbia, SC
30 January 2025

53036252R00102